BOHER

Forever Young

From Mod to Megastar: The Unofficial Rod Stewart Story

Copyright © 2025 by Bobby Gallagher

All rights reserved. No part of this publication may be reproduced, stored or transmitted in any form or by any means, electronic, mechanical, photocopying, recording, scanning, or otherwise without written permission from the publisher. It is illegal to copy this book, post it to a website, or distribute it by any other means without permission.

Bobby Gallagher asserts the moral right to be identified as the author of this work.

Bobby Gallagher has no responsibility for the persistence or accuracy of URLs for external or third-party Internet Websites referred to in this publication and does not guarantee that any content on such Websites is, or will remain, accurate or appropriate.

Designations used by companies to distinguish their products are often claimed as trademarks. All brand names and product names used in this book and on its cover are trade names, service marks, trademarks and registered trademarks of their respective owners. The publishers and the book are not associated with any product or vendor mentioned in this book. None of the companies referenced within the book have endorsed the book.

First edition

This book was professionally typeset on Reedsy. Find out more at reedsy.com

Contents

1	Introduction: The Gospel According to Rod the Mod	1
2	Reason to Believe	5
3	Handbags and Gladrags	10
4	Good Morning Little Schoolboy	15
5	Gasoline Alley Dreams	20
6	Stay With Me	24
7	Every Picture Told a Story	28
8	You Wear It Well	32
9	Do Ya Think He's Sexy?	36
10	Sailing	41
11	Young Turks & Wild Hearts	46
12	The First Cut Is the Deepest	51
13	Tonight's the Night	56
14	Some Guys Have All the Luck	61
15	Forever Young	66
16	Rhythm of My Heart	70
17	Handbags & Gladrags	75
18	Sailing	79
19	This Old Heart of Mine	84
20	Baby Jane	88
21	You're in My Heart	92
22	Fan Fun	96

23	Thank You (for the Music, the Hair, and the Heart)	99
24	Rod Stewart Discography	101

1

Introduction: The Gospel According to Rod the Mod

"**You can't say I ain't lived.**" – **Rod Stewart**

I've never worn leopard print with confidence. Not for lack of trying - I've owned three leopard shirts, one zebra scarf, and a pair of tartan trousers that scared my neighbours and confused my cat. But when Rod Stewart wears animal print, the world says, "Now *that's* fashion." When I do it, people ask if I've come from a fancy-dress party. That, dear reader, is the magic of Rod the Mod.

This book is a love letter. Not the kind he used to leave tucked under pillows in LA hotel suites, but the type written by a lifelong fan - someone who's air-sung *Sailing* in the bath, belted out *Maggie May* in traffic, and cried over *The First Cut Is the Deepest* more than once. I didn't choose Rod Stewart. He chose me - or at least, his voice did. One raspy verse at a time.

I was about ten years old when I first heard that unmistakable growl - part gravel, part honey, all heart - coming through the car stereo. My mum was a Rod girl. Still is. She had the *Greatest Hits* cassette on constant rotation, wedged into our clunky Ford Fiesta with a biro to rewind it when it got stuck. "This one's about a woman who left him," she'd say, as if that narrowed it down. But I remember that feeling, that first jolt of something real. He wasn't just singing. He was *bleeding.* And it sounded beautiful.

This wasn't just pop music. This was soul and sweat and swagger, all tangled up in melody. I didn't understand half of what he was saying, but I knew it *meant* something. I knew he meant it. And that's been Rod's magic trick for more than six decades: making you believe it - every kiss-off, every yearning chorus, every cheeky wink hidden between the lines.

So why write this book?

Because Rod Stewart is more than a chart-topper. He's a cultural institution with spiky hair and a glint in his eye. Because too often, when we talk about icons, Rod gets lumped in as the guy who wore tight trousers and dated models. And yes - he *did* do that (and often). But there's so much more behind the headlines and hair gel. There's poetry in his path. There's craft in that chaos. And there's a legacy in those love songs, one that deserves to be shouted about from the rooftops of Glasgow to the Vegas Strip.

This book is unofficial, unfiltered, and unashamedly fan-written. It's not just about the records and the romances, though we'll have plenty of those. It's about the journey - how a working-class lad from North London with a love of football and Sam Cooke records carved a path from smoky clubs to stadiums,

INTRODUCTION: THE GOSPEL ACCORDING TO ROD THE MOD

from heartbreak to knighthood. It's about reinvention. About resilience. About keeping your sense of humour even when the tabloids are dragging your name through yesterday's glitter.

Rod Stewart is, in many ways, the last of a certain kind of rock star. The type who could drink you under the table, charm your mum, steal your girlfriend, and still make you thank him for the experience. He's a romantic and a rascal, a showman with soul. And he's never stopped evolving - from blues to glam rock, disco to standards, he's always one step ahead, even when he's dancing two steps behind in tight white trousers.

Over the next twenty chapters, we'll walk the cobbled streets of Highgate and the glittering boulevards of Hollywood. We'll meet the Faces, the flames, and the football squads. We'll revisit the scandals, the setbacks, the comebacks, and the slow-dance ballads that made you cry after three gins. We'll explore what made him iconic - not just the hits, but the *heart* behind them.

Because here's the thing: Rod Stewart didn't become beloved by accident. It wasn't just

the hair (though let's be honest, the hair *helped*). It's that voice - full of ache and laughter. It's the way he writes women into anthems, the way he talks about his kids like they're the greatest gig he ever played. It's the fact that he still shows up, still sings like he means it, and still looks like he's having more fun than the rest of us combined.

This isn't a tale of rise and fall. It's a story of rise, rise again, and then build a model railway in your mansion and rise a bit more. Rod's been counted out more times than he can remember - by critics, by exes, even by himself - but he always comes back. Maybe not with a vengeance, but with a wink, a grin, and another chorus you'll hum for weeks.

So, if you're here for the gossip - yes, we'll talk about Britt and Rachel and Penny. If you're here for the music - oh, we'll go deep into the grooves, trust me. And if you're here because something about *You're in My Heart* made you feel less alone in your own love story? Then pour a drink, grab your fanciest scarf, and join me.

Because this is a biography with the volume turned up. It's Rod as he lived it - loud, lush, and full of feeling. I can't promise objectivity, but I *can* promise honesty. This is the story of a man who never stopped loving his audience, and of a fan who never stopped loving the man.

So come on - let's twist the mic stand, kick off the heels (or the brogues), and step into the spotlight. From mod beginnings to megastar brilliance, Rod Stewart's story is one worth singing.

And baby - he wears it *very* well.

2

Reason to Believe

"*If I listened long enough to you, I'd find a way to believe that it's all true.*" – *Reason to Believe*, **Rod Stewart**

There's always a moment - a blink-and-you-miss-it heartbeat in time - when someone goes from *almost* to *absolutely*. For Rod Stewart, that moment didn't happen on a stage, or in a recording studio, or even during a wild night in L.A. It happened, improbably, in a graveyard.

Highgate Cemetery, to be exact.

Before the champagne-soaked chart-toppers and silver-streaked mullet, before the stadium tours and knightly honours, Rod Stewart was just a lad from North London with a mop of dirty-blond hair, a chip on his shoulder, and a harmonica in his coat pocket. He was earning a few quid posing as a model for art students and digging graves with his old man on chilly Saturday mornings. It was dirty work. Honest work. And, as it turns out, poetic foreshadowing - because Rod was always going to bury the past to sing about the future.

Born Roderick David Stewart on January 10, 1945, the youngest of five, Rod grew up in a post-war Britain trying to stitch itself back together with tea, football, and quiet resolve. His father, Robert, was a stoic Scotsman and a master builder by trade. His mother, Elsie, kept the Stewart household humming in Highgate - all mismatched socks, hand-me-down dreams, and the kind of kitchen that always smelled like toast. Rod was doted on, the baby of the family, but even as a kid, he had the kind of energy that could knock furniture over just by entering the room.

He wasn't born with a microphone in his hand. In fact, for the longest time, the only stage he dreamed of standing on was a football pitch. He idolised Scottish centre-forwards and spent his school days dribbling through puddles and defending imaginary goals. He even tried to go pro, training briefly with Brentford Football Club. But as he later said, "I didn't have the dedication - or the legs." The game's loss was music's gain.

Rod's real musical education came not in the classroom, but through the family record player. While other kids were digging Cliff Richard, Rod was falling hard for Sam Cooke. That voice - so smooth, so vulnerable, so *human* - planted something deep in Rod's gut. Add in a bit of Otis Redding, a dash of Little Richard, and that trusty harmonica he took everywhere, and you had the raw ingredients for what would soon become one of rock's most unforgettable voices.

He wasn't quite sure how to begin, though. London's music scene in the early '60s was a chaotic cocktail of mod fashion, pub gigs, and enough denim to clothe a small country. Rod floated through it all like a street-smart dandy in search of a chorus. He tried his hand with a few fledgling groups - The Ray Davies Quartet (yes, *that* Ray Davies), Jimmy Powell and the Five Dimensions, and a stint with Long John Baldry's Hoochie Coochie Men. Each step gave him a bit more swagger, a bit more certainty that maybe - just maybe - there was a stage out there with his name on it.

But it wasn't always glamour. There were train rides that ended nowhere, gigs where the only audience was a drunk with a toothpick, and more rejection than most young men could stomach. Yet Rod had something most didn't: a voice that sounded like a gravel driveway dipped in honey, and a grin that could disarm even the frostiest A&R man.

That voice, though - that was the game-changer. It didn't sound polished. It didn't sound trained. It sounded *real*. When Rod sang, you didn't just hear it - you *felt* it. It was the sound of someone who'd been dumped and danced in the same night. It was hopeful. It was heartbreaking. And it didn't sound like anyone else.

His first big break came in 1967 when he joined the Jeff Beck Group as lead vocalist. It was there that the true Rod began to emerge - not just the singer, but the *performer*. Touring the States with Beck's searing guitar licks behind him, Rod learned how to work a crowd, how to command a stage, how to let the music crash over you like a wave and come up gasping, fists in the air.

It wasn't easy. Jeff Beck was brilliant, but volatile. And Rod - still figuring himself out - often found himself caught between admiration and anxiety. Still, those years were formative. They taught him about grit. About power. About the kind of rock 'n' roll that left your ears ringing and your soul stirred.

By the time the Jeff Beck Group began to fracture, Rod had already caught the eye of some key players in the London music scene. That voice - that *face* - was too good to ignore. He joined up with the remnants of Small Faces (newly renamed *Faces*) and suddenly, Rod the solo artist was blossoming alongside Rod the band frontman. Two parallel tracks - one wild and whiskey-soaked, the other melodic and soul-baring - began to define his dual identity.

And it was during this exact time that something else happened: Rod started to believe in himself.

There's a reason *Reason to Believe* became such a signature track. It's not just the title - it's the message. Rod Stewart, in those early years, was always chasing something. Chasing sound. Chasing style. Chasing acceptance. But once he realised that his imperfections were *the thing* - that his raspy delivery, his everyman charm, his blend of raw and romantic was *the brand* - the game changed.

He stopped chasing and started *owning*. And when that happened, the world caught up.

By the end of the decade, Rod wasn't just a promising talent. He was a rising star. The grave-digging football hopeful was becoming rock's most unlikely heartthrob. And all because he believed - not in the industry, not in the hype, but in the power of his voice to tell the truth, even when it hurt.

So if you've ever wondered how a skinny North London lad with second-hand boots and a secondhand harmonica wound up on magazine covers, singing to millions, and getting knighted by the Queen... well, this is where it begins.

In the grit. In the grind. In the reason to believe.

3

Handbags and Gladrags

"**Ever seen a blind man cross the road, tryin' to make it to the other side?**" – *Handbags and Gladrags*, **Rod Stewart**

Clothes, they say, make the man. In Rod Stewart's case, they made the myth.

If Chapter One was about finding the voice, then Chapter Two is about finding the *look* - and Rod, bless him, didn't stumble into it accidentally. He *chose* to stand out. In a world still draped in post-war grays and buttoned-up conformity, he draped himself in velvet, eyeliner, and electric patterns that made your nan faint. This wasn't vanity. This was war paint.

Rod Stewart grew up in a family where clothing meant function. His father was a builder. His brothers were footballers and tradesmen. Practical. Solid. Dependable. Rod? Rod was the kid stealing his sisters' scarves and turning up his shirt collars. He didn't want to be solid - he wanted to be *seen*. And when Mod culture swept through London in the early '60s, he saw his tribe.

Mods were everything Rod craved: stylish, sharp, defiant. They dressed like they had somewhere expensive to be, even if they were skint. Tailored suits, desert boots, motor scooters - fashion as rebellion. And Rod, with his cheekbones and that mess of wheat-blond hair, slipped right in.

He wasn't rich. Far from it. But Mod culture taught him something crucial: *you didn't need money to have class.* All you needed was confidence, a good tailor (or at least a decent secondhand shop), and the guts to wear something louder than your voice. Rod made thrift stores look like Carnaby Street catwalks. He raided Portobello Road stalls like they were treasure chests and found magic in paisley.

He didn't just wear clothes. He *performed* them.

And that was the difference. Plenty of musicians had style. Rod had *flair.* He could make a velvet jacket look like a crown, a feather boa seem like armour. Where other lads dressed up for the weekend, Rod lived like he was perpetually en route to a Vogue cover shoot via the local pub.

But it wasn't just about standing out. It was about standing for something. Fashion, for Rod, was freedom. In a time when expectations were rigid - men in one box, women in another, everyone trying to fit - Rod was blurring the lines. He didn't care if his trousers were too tight or his shirts too sheer. He looked good. He *felt* good. And if you didn't like it, you could take your pint and your prejudice elsewhere.

Still, this wasn't just vanity on parade. Rod's sense of style was inseparable from his musical identity. He knew that when you walked onstage, the first thing people saw wasn't your soul - it was your silhouette. And Rod's silhouette was unforgettable: skinny hips, feathered hair, long scarves trailing behind him like a comet. You didn't need to hear a note to know this bloke was a star.

The music press at the time didn't always get it. They liked their rockers rugged, dirty, and denim-clad. Rod, with his lipstick and lace, made them nervous. He wasn't one of the boys. He was something else entirely - glam before glam, a rock 'n' roll romantic who dressed like he was in love with his own legend.

But fans? They loved it. Women wanted him. Men wanted to be him (or at least borrow his jacket). And Rod, ever the showman, leaned into it with glee. He took style risks because he understood something essential: music is theatre, and every outfit is a scene change.

And yet, for all the flash and fabulousness, Rod never lost his roots. Even when draped in satin and sequins, there was always a glint of the working-class lad who dug graves and idolised footballers. His outfits might scream Paris runway, but his grin said North London mischief. That tension - that blend of swagger and sincerity - became his trademark.

"Handbags and Gladrags," the Mike d'Abo-penned ballad Rod recorded early in his solo career, says everything about this chapter of his life. It's a song about the hollowness of material things - a warning against chasing style at the cost of substance. And Rod, ever the emotional alchemist, made it *ache*. Because for all his fashion-forward dazzle, he knew that style without soul was just costume.

In those years, Rod didn't just dress the part - he *became* it. The tousled hair, the eyeliner, the endless parade of patterned blazers - it wasn't fakery. It was him, fully realised, at a time when most people were still trying to figure out how to tie a cravat.

He wasn't following trends. He was *setting* them.

By the time he joined The Jeff Beck Group, he was already known around Soho for his distinctive look. People clocked him on the street not as "that guy with the harmonica," but "that bloke who looks like a pop star." He could make an entrance just by walking into a chip shop. And when he opened his mouth to sing? Forget it. The look and the voice collided like fireworks.

Years later, Rod would still talk about those early Mod days with affection. Not just for the clothes, but for what they represented. Youth. Rebellion. Identity. The right to be *more*. For Rod Stewart, style wasn't about hiding behind something. It was about stepping into who you really were - louder, bolder, and unafraid.

And maybe that's the point. Rod didn't wear those clothes to impress anyone. He wore them to *become* someone. Someone bigger. Someone freer. Someone who didn't just walk down the street - he *strutted*. And in doing so, he gave the rest of us permission to strut a little too.

So if you've ever hesitated before slipping into something too shiny, too bold, too *you* - think of Rod. Think of the boy in the secondhand blazer with stars in his eyes and a scarf trailing in the wind.

And wear it well.

4

Good Morning Little Schoolboy

"**Good morning, little schoolgirl, can I go home with you?**" – *Good Morning Little Schoolgirl*, **Rod Stewart** (1964)

Before the world called him Rod the Mod, he was just Rod the New Kid - the bloke with the harmonica, the jagged hair, and a dream too big for Highgate. He wasn't famous. He wasn't rich. He certainly wasn't knighted. But he was *ready*. And like any hungry young singer in 1960s London, he knew that if you wanted a break, you had to make noise - preferably while carrying your own amp on the Tube.

Rod Stewart's first taste of being a frontman didn't come in a smoky club or at some glamorous audition. It came in the cramped back rooms of record shops, music stores, and anywhere else he could corner someone who looked like they owned a microphone. His earliest gigs were more ragtag than rockstar - often paid in beer or bus fare, occasionally not at all. Still, he showed up. He *always* showed up.

In 1962, he picked up his first real on-stage experience with a group called The Ray Davies Quartet - yes, *that* Ray Davies, who would later go on to form The Kinks. But Rod didn't stick around long. It wasn't a love match. The band was green, the sound not quite right. More importantly, Rod hadn't yet found the thing that made his voice make sense. His influences were deeply rooted in American soul and blues, but no one was handing out record deals to London boys singing Sam Cooke covers in a Cockney twang.

He needed a band. He needed direction. He needed to sound like *himself*.

What he found, initially, was a rotating cast of almosts. In 1963, he joined Jimmy Powell and the Five Dimensions, a middling R&B outfit looking for a bit of edge. Rod sang backup and played harmonica, occasionally getting shoved to the front when the set needed some razzle. It wasn't glamorous. But it was a step - a rung on the ladder he was willing to crawl up, one blistered fingertip at a time.

Then came Long John Baldry - six feet seven inches of blues authority, with a booming voice and a bigger presence. Baldry spotted Rod busking one night at Twickenham Station, belting out "Smokestack Lightning" with all the conviction of a man who had nowhere to sleep but knew how to sing. Baldry, ever the talent scout, offered him a gig on the spot. Just like that, Rod had his in.

Joining Baldry's *Hoochie Coochie Men* wasn't just a step forward - it was a jolt. The gigs were real. The band had a following. And Rod finally had a chance to sing lead, in front of real crowds, with real musicians backing him. This was where his voice - that sandpaper croon, part bluesman, part bus stop busker - started to find its home. It wasn't polished. It wasn't precise. But it *moved* people.

Still, Rod didn't quite fit the blues purist mould. Baldry was from the school of slow-burning, formal authenticity - tight suits and reverent nods to the Chicago legends. Rod, on the other hand, wanted to shake the walls. He was more showman than scholar. After a few spirited disagreements, he moved on again.

Next came *Steampacket*, a so-called "supergroup" before supergroups were even a thing. Alongside Baldry, future solo star Julie Driscoll, and organist Brian Auger, Rod toured the UK with a fiery mix of soul, jazz, and R&B. But the band was too crowded, too democratic. Everyone had a mic. Everyone wanted the spotlight. And Rod? Well, he was ready to stop sharing.

In 1964, he recorded his very first solo single - a cover of "Good Morning Little Schoolgirl." It didn't set the charts on fire. In fact, it barely flickered. But there was something in it - a brashness, a hunger - that felt unmistakably *him*. Rod wasn't trying to be Sam Cooke anymore. He was trying to be Rod Stewart. The first, the only.

Even as the gigs improved, Rod remained a man in motion. He played with a blur of groups whose names now read like pub quiz trivia: Shotgun Express, The Soul Agents, The Dimensions (again), and more. Some folded. Some fired him. Some just faded out. But Rod never stopped. The voice kept getting better. The suits kept getting louder. And somewhere in that mess of sound and sweat, a star was starting to flicker.

By the mid-60s, London's music scene was eating itself alive -

rock was turning into blues was turning into soul was turning into something no one could name. Rod was at the center of it all. Not quite famous. Not quite broke. Just *circling*, like a dog waiting for the front door to open.

And then came the door - a six-string-shaped one, held open by Jeff Beck.

Rod had met Jeff Beck in passing, as most musicians in London did - at parties, backstage, inside music shops. Beck had just left The Yardbirds and was building a new band: loud, wild, and totally unhinged. He needed a singer who could roar over his guitar like a jet engine. He needed someone who could sell emotion without sanding it down. He needed *Rod*.

Rod was hesitant. Beck was intimidating, prone to mood swings, and known for chasing perfection to the point of madness. But the offer was too good to refuse. In 1967, Rod joined The Jeff Beck Group as lead vocalist. It was the biggest gamble of his career - and the beginning of everything.

With Beck on guitar and Rod on vocals, the band sounded like nothing else. Raw. Dirty.

Electric. It was the sound of blues reimagined through a British back alley. They toured the US, blew minds, and laid the groundwork for what would become heavy metal, punk, and glam rock in one fell swoop. Audiences who'd never heard of Rod Stewart walked away converted. That voice - that *voice* - turned heads from New York to San Francisco.

For Rod, it was validation. All those pub gigs, all those cheap suits, all those nearly-made-its had led to this. He was no longer just a harmonica player with good hair. He was *the voice*. And people were finally listening.

It hadn't been quick. It hadn't been easy. But as Rod himself might say - you've got to pay your dues before you wear the crown.

And baby, his crown was waiting.

5

Gasoline Alley Dreams

"**I** think I'll pack my bags and move on, move on..." – *Gasoline Alley*, **Rod Stewart**

There's something beautifully ironic about Rod Stewart's early 1970s: just as his solo star was beginning to shine, he joined a band where he was technically *not* the frontman. A band that ran on booze, brotherhood, and pure, unapologetic chaos. A band where the amplifier might catch fire mid-song, and nobody would blink. A band called *The Faces*.

To understand Rod in the '70s, you have to understand *The Faces* - not just as a band, but as a lifestyle. They weren't The Rolling Stones. They weren't chasing elegance or critical respect. They were chasing the next pint, the next solo, the next stage that hadn't yet banned them. And into this mix came Rod, the stylish ex-busker with a growing solo career and a voice like gravel being poured over gold.

Let's back up a minute.

By 1969, The Jeff Beck Group had imploded - too much ego,

too little oxygen. Rod was frustrated, exhausted, and not yet famous enough to call the shots. But there was a silver lining. With Beck out of the picture, Rod found himself musically adrift - and drifting straight into the arms of a band on the brink of reinvention.

The Small Faces - once fronted by the electric Steve Marriott - were in limbo. Marriott had left to form Humble Pie, and the remaining members were looking for a new direction. Enter Rod Stewart, and his Jeff Beck Group mate, Ronnie Wood. The timing was perfect. The chemistry? Instant.

Renaming themselves *The Faces*, the band became a kind of rock 'n' roll family - loud, scruffy, deeply talented, and occasionally capable of miracles. Ron Wood's guitar was loose and soulful, Ronnie Lane's bass was as melodic as it was muddy, Ian McLagan's keyboards were pure pub joy, and Kenny Jones on drums hit like he was settling a score.

And then there was Rod.

Officially, The Faces were a democratic unit - no one was the star, no one the boss. But let's be honest: the moment Rod stepped up to the mic, it was *his* show. That voice. That swagger. That shock of hair that seemed to defy both gravity and good sense. Rod wasn't just in the band - he *became* the band's heartbeat.

But here's the kicker: it *worked*. Rod didn't dominate The Faces - he *belonged* to them. For all his polish and poise, he found something in that band he hadn't yet discovered as a solo artist: camaraderie. They were scrappy and gloriously unrefined. They drank too much. They missed cues. They occasionally fell over. But they loved each other. And that love spilled out onto the stage in a way that was magnetic.

Their live shows were legendary - not always for the tightness of the music, but for the sheer *joy* of it. Faces concerts felt like house parties where someone happened to plug in a few guitars. Rod would swing the mic stand like a lasso, Ronnie Wood would solo for ten minutes too long, and no one - not the band, not the audience - would want it any other way.

And yet, amidst the beer-soaked debauchery, they made real music. Albums like *First Step* (1970), *Long Player* (1971), and *A Nod Is As Good As a Wink... to a Blind Horse* (1971) weren't always critical darlings, but they contained moments of pure magic. Songs like "Stay With Me" - swaggering, suggestive, irresistible - became FM radio staples. Others, like "Debris" and "Love Lives Here," hinted at a depth beneath the denim.

Rod, for his part, was living a double life. While The Faces were barrelling across stages in a haze of amp feedback and lager fumes, his solo career was quietly exploding. *An Old Raincoat Won't Ever Let You Down* (1969) and *Gasoline Alley* (1970) showed a softer, more introspective Rod - the romantic, the storyteller, the balladeer.

Gasoline Alley, in particular, was a turning point. The title track, with its bittersweet lyrics and gentle acoustic textures, felt like the heart of a man looking back at his youth with equal parts affection and regret. It was Rod's London - all cobbled alleys and fading streetlights - set to music. And fans *felt* it.

That tension - between the band's rowdy energy and his solo sensitivity - would define Rod in the early '70s. He was playing two characters at once: the roughneck frontman and the poetic heartbreaker. And the wild thing is... he was *brilliant* at both.

But cracks began to show. The more successful Rod's solo career became - especially after *Every Picture Tells a Story* and the juggernaut hit "Maggie May" - the more he was pulled away from the band that had become his family. Faces gigs started feeling like Rod Stewart concerts with guests. Press began to focus on him alone. The other members noticed.

Tensions rose. Ronnie Lane, in particular, resented the imbalance. What had started as a band of brothers was turning into a one-man show with a backing group - and Rod, whether he meant to or not, was drifting toward the spotlight.

Still, for a few glorious years, The Faces and Rod Stewart created something rare: chaos with chemistry, mess with meaning. They reminded the world that rock music didn't have to be perfect - it just had to be *real*. And when Rod sang, eyes closed, clutching the mic like it was the last thing keeping him tethered to Earth, you believed every word.

Gasoline Alley was more than an album title. It was a state of mind - nostalgic, rebellious, hopeful. For Rod, it captured the moment he stopped being a working musician and started becoming a rock icon.

And even if the alley was rough, even if the dreams were blurry, he was already moving on.

6

Stay With Me

"**I**n the morning, don't say you love me - 'cause I'll only kick you out of the door." – *Stay With Me*, The Faces

There's a sound that came out of Rod Stewart's mouth in 1971 that changed the trajectory of his entire life. A voice cracking open on the line *"Wake up, Maggie, I think I got something to say to you..."* - unpolished, unscripted, utterly unforgettable. That song - "Maggie May" - wasn't supposed to be the hit. It was the B-side. The afterthought. But the world had other plans.

Suddenly, Rod Stewart wasn't just a singer. He was *the voice* of a generation trying to sound confident while still bleeding from the heart. And while *Maggie* made him a household name, another song - *"Stay With Me"* - cemented the myth.

Let's talk about that dichotomy.

On one side: "Maggie May" - the wistful, wounded anthem about an older woman and a boy too young to know better. It was raw, autobiographical, and packed with regret. Rod wrote it about a real encounter (ahem, *experience*) with a woman who taught him as much about loss as she did about love. The lyrics weren't polished poetry. They were *honest* - stammering, stumbling, emotionally naked. And that's why they hit so hard.

On the other: "Stay With Me" - the barroom brawler of a track that swaggered onto the scene like it owned the jukebox. Written with Ronnie Wood for The Faces, it was fast, flirtatious, and not remotely subtle. A woman comes home. A one-night stand is suggested. She's warned not to overstay. The tone? Equal parts cheeky and chauvinistic. But here's the kicker - it worked. Because Rod didn't just sing it - he *winked* through it. He made sleaze sound like theatre.

Both songs came out around the same time. Both became anthems. And together, they captured the two Rods the world was falling in love with: the romantic and the rascal.

Let's start with "Maggie May."

Released as part of the *Every Picture Tells a Story* album, "Maggie" wasn't even intended as the lead single. But when radio DJs started flipping the record and playing it instead of "Reason to Believe," the phones lit up. Listeners wanted *that* voice. That story. That brutal honesty wrapped in mandolin and melancholy. Within weeks, it topped the charts in both the UK and US. Rod had gone from cult favourite to global star in a single season.

He was *everywhere*. Magazine covers. TV specials. Stadium stages. And with that fame came a new kind of scrutiny - and chaos.

Rod, ever the multitasker, was now juggling two full careers:

solo artist and Faces frontman. But things were starting to tilt. His solo work was polished, poignant, praised. The Faces? Still delightfully drunk, still occasionally brilliant, still teetering on the edge of collapse.

Tensions grew backstage. Faces shows were being swarmed not for the band, but for *Rod*. Fans screamed his name, shoved their way to the front, brought signs and bras and tear-streaked declarations of devotion. Rod took it in stride - he'd always liked attention - but the strain was obvious. The brotherhood was cracking.

Rod's style evolved too. The early '70s Rod was still a bit scrappy - boots, scarves, open shirts. But as the spotlight grew, so did the sparkle. Sequins crept in. Platforms got higher. His hair took on a life of its own. He became not just a singer, but a *star*. A performer. A *phenomenon*.

And with fame came... women.

Rod's love life during this era is the stuff of legend. Tall blondes, French actresses, models draped over his shoulder like boas - the tabloids couldn't get enough. But while the public lapped it up, Rod was rarely cruel about it. Yes, there were flings. Yes, there were missteps. But he spoke of women with awe, not ownership. He was the boy forever amazed that the girl actually *said yes*.

Still, songs like "Stay With Me" did him no favours with feminists. The lyrics were bold - borderline brash - and critics raised eyebrows. But fans knew the truth: Rod was playing a part. He wasn't mocking women - he was mocking *himself*. That rogue persona? It was as much theatre as it was autobiography. A lad on the prowl, sure, but one with a self-aware smirk.

Behind the scenes, though, the pressures were mounting. Rod wanted to be loyal to The Faces - they were his mates, his brothers, his band. But his solo career was outpacing theirs at warp speed. Record execs were focusing their budgets and marketing on *Rod Stewart*, not the collective. Tours became more Rod-focused. And as the gap widened, the love frayed.

Rod later said that during this time, he was the loneliest he'd ever been. Surrounded by people, worshipped by fans, but unsure where he belonged. The boy who wanted to be in a band was now being pulled toward becoming a brand. And while his name was shining in lights, something about that shift quietly broke his heart.

Still, the hits kept coming. "You Wear It Well," "Twistin' the Night Away," "I'd Rather Go Blind" - he was a machine, churning out classics with the voice of a man who sounded like he'd lived five lifetimes in a smoky pub.

And yet, the dream was becoming unsustainable. Faces would limp through another couple of albums and tours, but by 1975, the writing was on the wall. Rod was no longer the lead singer of a band. He was a solo artist, full stop.

But in 1971 - the year of *Maggie May* and *Stay With Me* - he was both. He was heartbreaker and hitmaker, poet and player. He was everything all at once.

And the world, bless it, couldn't get enough.

7

Every Picture Told a Story

"**E**very picture tells a story, don't it?" – *Every Picture Tells a Story*, **Rod Stewart**

By 1971, Rod Stewart had more than a few stories to tell - and not just the kind that ended in hotel rooms or hungover breakfasts. He had tales of heartbreak, brotherhood, ambition, and the aching in-between moments that don't make the headlines but live forever in your voice. *Every Picture Tells a Story* wasn't just the name of his third solo album - it was a *mission statement*. A declaration. A growl and a grin rolled into one.

Up to this point, Rod had been known for *having* a voice. But with this album, he proved he also had *something to say*.

Let's start with the basics: *Every Picture Tells a Story* came out in May 1971, just months before *Maggie May* would accidentally take over the world. But the album was already a landmark. It was the sound of Rod Stewart without compromise - raw, unfussy, full of instinct. Produced on a shoestring, recorded in spare sessions between Faces gigs, and stitched together by Rod, Ron Wood, and a handful of trusted hands, it was as scrappy as it was sublime.

The title track – "Every Picture Tells a Story" – sets the tone from the first crack of the snare. It's part spoken word, part gospel-blues gallop. Rod doesn't so much sing as *confess*, rambling through stories of travel, women, rejection, and spiritual discovery like a rock 'n' roll Jack Kerouac. It's messy, episodic, and wildly magnetic. The song takes detours, falls down, gets back up – just like the life it's describing.

What makes it special is how unfiltered it feels. There's no sense of industry polish here. Rod isn't performing for the charts – he's emptying his pockets and showing you the receipts. You get the sense that if the tape had kept rolling, he'd have kept going.

And then, of course, there's *Maggie May*.

We've already talked about it – the chance hit, the B-side that outshone everything – but in the context of this album, it's devastating. Nestled between ramshackle rockers and folky experiments, "Maggie May" is *real*. The mandolin line, played by Ray Jackson of Lindisfarne, was an afterthought. The vocal take was imperfect. The lyrics, written from a bruised and confused heart, had Rod worried they were too personal. But it was *exactly* that rawness that made it a masterpiece.

It's not just about a woman. It's about *growing up*. About losing innocence and still loving the one who took it. And Rod sings it like he's barely holding it together – not crying, but almost. It's not a performance. It's a reckoning.

Other standouts on the album prove just how wide Rod's reach really was. "Mandolin Wind" – tender and windblown – is one of his most underrated tracks, a quietly devastating ballad that shows how deeply he could feel when the stage lights dimmed. "I Know I'm Losing You," originally by The Temptations, is turned into a thunderous stomp with The Faces backing him in full swagger mode.

And then there's "(Find a) Reason to Believe" – a gentle, aching cover of the Tim Hardin song that had originally been pegged as the single. Rod's version drips with sincerity. It's a fitting closer, because if there's one thread running through *Every Picture Tells a Story*, it's *belief*. Belief in yourself, in your past, in your ability to turn scars into songs.

The album was a sensation. Critics loved it. Fans devoured it. And Rod, who had spent years scraping for recognition, suddenly found himself staring down the barrel of *global* fame.

He'd made two albums before this – *An Old Raincoat Won't Ever Let You Down* (1969) and *Gasoline Alley* (1970) – both solid, soulful affairs. But *Every Picture* was something different. It didn't just showcase Rod's voice. It captured his *essence*. The parts that were messy, sensitive, funny, bruised, and brilliant – they were all in there, track by track.

Rod had always admired storytellers. He was obsessed with Sam Cooke, Dylan, Otis – artists who didn't just sing *well*, but sang *true*. With *Every Picture*, Rod joined their ranks. He didn't need a chorus to stick in your head. He just needed a moment - a lyric, a turn of phrase, a groan in the right place - to rip your heart open.

What's even more impressive is how *lo-fi* the whole thing was. This wasn't a big-budget affair. They recorded some of it in spare studio time, patched things together with odd session players, and didn't fuss with multiple takes. But that was the point. The album wasn't supposed to be perfect. It was supposed to be *real*.

Rod later said he never wanted to make another record like it - not because he didn't love it, but because it was lightning in a bottle. A one-time thing. A fluke, maybe. But a glorious one.

It also marked the moment when Rod Stewart stepped out of *The Faces'* shadow - or maybe more accurately, when he started casting one of his own. As much as he loved the band (and he *did*), this album made it clear that he had stories to tell that didn't fit inside the barroom brawls and boys' club camaraderie of his bandmates. He needed space. He needed *scope*.

Rod Stewart, solo artist, had arrived.

And not quietly.

8

You Wear It Well

"*I* had nothing to do on this hot afternoon, but to settle down and write you a line." – *You Wear It Well*, Rod Stewart

By 1972, Rod Stewart wasn't just telling stories – he was *living* them. And he was doing it with a wardrobe that could make Liberace blush and a voice that still sounded like it had been dragged through a Soho alley and handed a whisky. "You Wear It Well" wasn't just a song – it was a metaphor. Rod was wearing *everything* well. The fame. The heartbreak. The pressure. The leopard-print suits. And somehow, he made it all look effortless.

Let's be clear: "You Wear It Well" is one of Rod's finest moments. Not because it reinvented the wheel, but because it didn't *try* to. It was a natural successor to "Maggie May" – same loose acoustic strumming, same wistful voice cracking under the weight of regret, same deeply British sense of humour hiding beneath the heartbreak. But where "Maggie" had been full of confusion and ache, "You Wear It Well" had a wink in its eye.

It was about love lost, sure - but it was also about loving the *memory* of love.

Written with Martin Quittenton (the same guitarist behind "Maggie"), the song came out on *Never a Dull Moment*, Rod's 1972 solo follow-up to *Every Picture Tells a Story*. It was another album recorded mostly with his Faces bandmates, under budget, and under the radar - a method that by now was almost *intentional*. Rod didn't like overproducing. He liked things to breathe, to break a little, to feel like a warm-up in a pub that just *happened* to be brilliant.

"You Wear It Well" opens with a letter - or at least, something close to one. It's written to an ex, a woman who's long gone but very much *alive* in the lines. Rod's narrator rambles through anecdotes and apologies, his voice equal parts charm and choke. He remembers birthdays missed, dresses worn, things unsaid. It's romantic, but also self-aware. "I made the best of what I had," he sings - and for a moment, you feel like he's not just singing to her, but to *us*.

That song, like the album it came from, marked a shift. Rod wasn't just the raspy lad with great hair and a cheeky grin anymore. He was becoming something deeper - a chronicler of grown-up feelings, of aging out of bravado, of missing people you once thought you'd always have. And he was doing it in a way that men weren't really *allowed* to do at the time. Vulnerability in rock? That was risky business. But Rod didn't flinch.

The rest of *Never a Dull Moment* built on this evolution. It had the same shaggy charm as its predecessor - rough edges, rambling solos, off-the-cuff production - but it also leaned more into blues and soul. There's his cover of Jimi Hendrix's "Angel," delivered like a gospel hymn on a hangover. There's "Twistin' the Night Away," reworked from Sam Cooke's original into a full-bodied stomp. There's even a cover of Etta James's "I'd Rather Go Blind" - and Rod doesn't just cover it, he *inhabits* it. The pain is palpable. The restraint is masterful.

What these songs reveal is an artist who's learning when *not* to sing. Rod's greatest power wasn't his volume - it was his *tone*. He could hit you harder with a whisper than most singers could with a scream. And in 1972, he was refining that skill, learning how to pull back just enough to let the lyrics bruise you before the chorus patched you up again.

But while the music was maturing, Rod's life was still a blur of parties, press, and personal entanglements. The tabloids couldn't get enough - and to be fair, Rod wasn't exactly hiding. He'd embraced his reputation as a womanizer, dressing the part and playing the role. He dated high-profile beauties, gave legendary interviews, and kept one foot firmly planted in the world of spectacle.

Yet the contradiction was always there - the rogue with the tender heart. Rod might sing about kicking a lover out in the morning, but he'd also write her a letter ten years later, just to say he still remembered the way she laughed. That push and pull - the rakish lothario and the romantic soul - made him fascinating. He wasn't pretending to be perfect. He was just being *honest*. And fans adored him for it.

The press often misunderstood this duality. To them, Rod was either a genius or a joke. He was praised for his voice one week, mocked for his trousers the next. But Rod didn't seem to care.

He kept writing. Kept touring. Kept dressing like a rock 'n' roll matador. And he *wore it well*.

There's something else to note here, too - Rod's unique connection with his audience. While other stars cultivated mystery or danger, Rod felt like someone you *knew*. The guy from the pub. The bloke your sister dated. He was accessible, even when dressed like a peacock. And that relatability made his heartbreak songs hit even harder. When Rod sang about losing someone, it didn't feel like a rock star pining for a model. It felt like your mate, quietly hurting behind the banter.

"You Wear It Well" reached number one in the UK and cracked the top 20 in the US. It wasn't the cultural juggernaut that "Maggie May" had been, but it confirmed something vital: Rod Stewart wasn't a fluke. He wasn't a one-hit wonder, or a novelty, or a lucky pub singer with a gravelly voice. He was a *writer*. A *stylist*. A *storyteller*.

And with every verse, every outfit, every open vein he poured onto tape, he was building something. Not just a career - a *catalogue*. A body of work that would outlast fashion, fame, and even the Faces themselves.

So yes, he wore it well - the heartbreak, the humour, the hunger. And in doing so, he gave the rest of us a blueprint for how to move on with dignity, memory, and a little bit of swagger.

Because sometimes, love leaves you. But if you can sing about it like *this*?

You win anyway.

9

Do Ya Think He's Sexy?

I"f you want my body and you think I'm sexy, come on, sugar, let me know." – *Da Ya Think I'm Sexy?*, Rod Stewart

Rod Stewart had always been sexy. Just ask the sea of screaming fans, the piles of love letters, or the ever-rotating cast of women hanging on his arm in tabloid spreads. But in 1978, he did something even bolder than asking the world to notice - he *asked out loud.*

And with that immortal line - *"If you want my body and you think I'm sexy..."* - Rod Stewart set fire to every expectation the music world had about him. He traded tweed for satin, bluesy ballads for disco beats, and the smoky pub for Studio 54. And if the critics didn't like it? Well... they weren't invited to the party.

Let's set the stage.

By the late '70s, Rod was at the peak of his commercial powers.

He was selling out arenas, topping charts, and racking up platinum albums like he used to rack up speeding tickets. He could have stayed safe - made another heartfelt ballad, recorded a soulful cover, kept the mandolin man on speed dial.

But Rod Stewart has never been one to sit still.

Inspired by the disco scene that had taken over New York and London - and perhaps wanting to prove he could do *anything* - Rod co-wrote "Da Ya Think I'm Sexy?" with drummer Carmine Appice and keyboardist Duane Hitchings. They cooked up a synth-driven, four-on-the-floor monster that sounded nothing like "Maggie May" or "You Wear It Well" - and everything like a man who was ready to dominate the dancefloor.

The result? A global smash. The song shot to number one in the US, UK, Canada, Australia - practically everywhere with a functioning radio. It sold millions. It earned him a Grammy nomination. It played in clubs, weddings, shopping centres, and basements. Even your nan probably sang along once. Maybe twice.

And yet... *oh*, the backlash.

Rod, the man who had once personified rock authenticity, was now being accused of selling out. Critics were savage. Old fans were confused. Rolling Stone called it "an embarrassment." Serious musicians scoffed. Disco purists thought it was derivative. Rock purists thought it was betrayal. No one quite knew what to do with a man who used to sing about heartbreak now wiggling his hips to a Moog synthesizer.

But here's the thing: Rod *knew* what he was doing.

That trademark wink? It's all over "Da Ya Think I'm Sexy?" It's not just a seduction anthem - it's a parody, too. A tongue-in-cheek look at the absurdity of glam, fame, and sex appeal. The music video, with Rod strutting around in leopard-print tights, wasn't just provocative - it was *funny*. He wasn't begging to be loved. He was *mocking* the very idea of being reduced to a body.

Rod later said, "It was a joke. The song was a bloody laugh - but nobody got it."

That didn't stop the money from rolling in. Nor did it stop Rod from embracing the new sound. His 1978 album *Blondes Have More Fun* - featuring the single - leaned heavily into the disco-rock fusion. It was a commercial triumph. Rod was now a fixture in a new era of pop stardom - glittering, global, and a bit ridiculous.

But make no mistake: beneath the disco ball, he was still Rod.

Songs like "Ain't Love a Bitch" and "Last Summer" reminded fans that the raspy romantic was still alive and well. Even in his flashiest era, Rod never entirely abandoned his emotional roots. He just gave them a new wardrobe. And a synthesizer.

Live, he turned into a showman of epic proportions. Outfits sparkled. Hair got bigger. Stages expanded. But what never changed was *the voice*. Rod could sing disco, but he still did it with that same grainy soul that made "Mandolin Wind" feel like a confession.

Of course, the disco flirtation came at a price. As the genre began to implode in the early '80s - think *Disco Demolition Night* and anti-disco backlash - Rod had to shift again. He couldn't dance forever. But that brief, shimmering moment in the late '70s was a testament to his greatest superpower: *adaptation*.

Rod Stewart was never one genre. He was never one look. He was a moving target. And that's why he survived - and thrived - when others faded.

Behind the scenes, Rod was also undergoing changes. He had moved to Los Angeles, soaked up American sun, and fully embraced celebrity. His relationships - notably with model Alana Hamilton, whom he would marry in 1979 - became media obsessions. His image morphed from scrappy rocker to full-blown icon of excess.

He played football with Elton John. Threw parties that made headlines. Got papped in outfits that looked like stolen curtains from Caesar's Palace. And through it all, he *kept laughing*. Rod never took himself too seriously - a rare gift in a world of stars puffed up with their own importance.

"Da Ya Think I'm Sexy?" may have upset the critics, but it captured something essential about Rod: his refusal to be boxed in. He could cry over Maggie, pine on "Reason to Believe," and still pull on spandex and make people dance. He was versatile. Shameless. Joyful.

And let's be honest: the song *slaps*.

Years later, it would be re-evaluated - as most misunderstood classics are. Covered, sampled, remixed. Even the critics began to soften. It wasn't just a disco track. It was *Rod's* disco track. A chapter in his career where he proved that he didn't just evolve – he did it with a smirk.

So, do we think he's sexy?

Yeah. But more than that – we think he's fearless.

10

Sailing

"**I am sailing, I am sailing, home again, 'cross the sea.**" – *Sailing*, **Rod Stewart**

For a man so often photographed on land - foot on monitor, mic stand in hand, tartan trousers blazing - it's one of life's quiet contradictions that Rod Stewart's biggest ballad is about the sea.

"*Sailing*" didn't just make people cry. It made them *feel*. It became a hymn for goodbyes, for hope, for coming home. In a catalogue stacked with swagger and seduction, "Sailing" stood out like a lighthouse in a storm - clear, bright, steady. And at its centre was Rod, not roaring, but *reaching*.

The song wasn't his. It had been written by Gavin Sutherland of The Sutherland Brothers in 1972, recorded in a modest folk-rock style. It was beautiful, but barely made a splash. Then Rod got hold of it.

At first, he didn't want to do it.

He thought it was too slow. Too soft. Too far from the raucous sound he'd built with The Faces, and too removed from the glam-rock strut he was wearing so well. But his longtime producer Tom Dowd saw the potential. Rod, reluctantly, recorded it - and promptly forgot about it.

Then it was released.

"Sailing", launched as the lead single from *Atlantic Crossing* in 1975, took on a life of its own. It reached number one in the UK, staying there for four weeks. It wasn't just a hit - it was a *phenomenon*. Played at funerals, weddings, military farewells, and Sunday afternoons with nothing but rain on the windows.

It became *the* Rod Stewart ballad. Not the most personal. Not the most technical. But the most *universal*. Everyone saw themselves in it - the longing, the search for connection, the dream of returning somewhere safe. And Rod sang it like he meant every word. His voice - usually so gritty, so full of bravado - became something else entirely: soft-edged, windblown, vulnerable.

The timing was perfect. *Atlantic Crossing* was already a major shift for Rod. He had left the UK (and The Faces) behind, moving to Los Angeles for tax reasons - a decision that didn't sit well with British tabloids, who branded him a sell-out. But musically, the move opened him up. The album was smoother, more American, drenched in soul and layered production. Rod was reinventing himself - not just in geography, but in tone.

The album title was a not-so-subtle nod to his journey: across the Atlantic, away from the band, toward a solo identity that would carry him through the next four decades. And "Sailing" was the emotional centrepiece - even if he didn't write it, it *felt* like autobiography.

Rod was sailing - from London to L.A., from group chaos to solo control, from rock bravado to balladry.

And the public responded. "Sailing" became more than a song. It became a national anthem for people who didn't have a national anthem that captured what they *felt*. It was played endlessly. Used in the BBC documentary *Sailor*. Reissued during the Falklands War as a tribute to troops. It echoed through loudspeakers in churches and council flats alike.

It didn't matter that Rod was living in a mansion in Beverly Hills when he recorded it. The song felt *grounded*, humble. It made him feel like one of us. And that's always been Rod's magic - the ability to sound like your mate from the pub, even when he's singing from a yacht.

But "Sailing" also marked a deeper evolution. Rod was growing up. Leaving behind the cheeky chappy image - at least in part - and leaning into something more timeless. Something that would serve him well as the years rolled on and the suits got sharper.

Not that he left the hits behind. *Atlantic Crossing* also gave us "Stone Cold Sober" and "Three Time Loser" - swaggering reminders that Rod still knew how to throw elbows in a chorus. But it was clear that the album, and the move to America, had broadened him. The sound was slicker, more expansive. The ballads were deeper. The voice? Still raw, but now wrapped in velvet.

Behind the scenes, life was changing too.

Rod had broken away from The Faces, who were slowly crumbling without him. His solo career was no longer running *alongside* the band - it *was* the focus. There were new pressures. Bigger stages. More money. More critics. And more moments alone.

Rod has always said that "Sailing" was never meant to be a statement. It was just a song. But maybe that's why it worked so well - because it *wasn't* calculated. It was emotional instinct. A simple melody, a simple lyric, and a man who understood that the hardest thing to do in music is to be *simple* and still move people.

And Rod moved us.

He still does.

Years later, "Sailing" would remain a fixture in his live shows. A moment of quiet in the middle of the party. The lighters-up ballad before the encore. It never failed to hush the crowd. Because everyone had someone they wanted to come home to. Everyone had someone they'd lost. Everyone was sailing toward something.

Rod might have been wearing gold lamé trousers, but when he sang "Sailing," he wasn't a rock star. He was just a man with a microphone, trying to find his way.

And isn't that what we all are?

11

Young Turks & Wild Hearts

"**Young hearts be free tonight. Time is on your side.**" – ***Young Turks*, Rod Stewart**

By 1981, Rod Stewart had everything a rock star could want - platinum albums, a mansion in Beverly Hills, designer wardrobes, supermodel girlfriends, and hair that still defied gravity. He was a household name, an international icon, and the proud owner of a voice that had soundtracked an entire generation's heartbreaks and hangovers.

But he also had something new: a *family*.

Rod, the eternal bachelor, was now a father. Alana Hamilton - actress, model, tabloid regular, and his wife as of 1979 - had given birth to their daughter Kimberly and, not long after, their son Sean. And while Rod didn't exactly hang up the leather trousers and settle into domestic bliss, there was no denying it: the times, they were a-changing.

And so was Rod.

Enter *Young Turks* - a synth-laced, speed-driven anthem of teenage escape and wide-eyed rebellion. Released in 1981 as the lead single from *Tonight I'm Yours*, the song didn't sound like anything Rod had done before. It had a dance beat. A bubbling keyboard line. A sense of *urgency*. Gone were the acoustic twangs and bluesy wails - this was the future, fast-forwarded and remixed for a new generation.

And yet, it worked.

"*Young Turks*" wasn't just a stylistic shift - it was Rod's message to a younger audience that he was *still listening*. The song told the story of Billy and Patti, two teenagers who run away from home in search of freedom, love, and a life of their own. It could've been a preachy cautionary tale. But in Rod's hands, it became a *celebration*. He wasn't scolding them. He was *cheering them on*.

"Don't let them put you down. Don't let them push you around," he sings. And for every young listener in 1981 trying to find their own place in the world, it felt like a lifeline - coming from a man old enough to know better, but still young enough to remember what it felt like.

The irony, of course, is that Rod *wasn't* young anymore - not by pop standards, anyway. He was in his mid-thirties, newly married (briefly), newly sober (occasionally), and deeply entrenched in the kind of fame that didn't leave much room for reflection. But with "Young Turks," he tapped into something timeless: the hunger for *more*.

And in many ways, the song mirrored his own life.

Rod had never done things the way others expected. He hadn't come up through the traditional ranks. He didn't sing like a choirboy or act like a statesman. He'd carved a path through grit, charm, talent, and sheer nerve. He was the original young Turk – defiant, restless, always one step ahead of the sound.

Tonight I'm Yours as an album followed suit. It was a sharp departure from the romantic ballads and raspy heartbreaks of the '70s. Synthesizers, drum machines, angular melodies – Rod was stepping into the '80s like he owned the decade already. Tracks like "Tora, Tora, Tora (Out with the Boys)" and the title song crackled with energy. Even the cover art – Rod bathed in bold, electric pink and blue – screamed transformation.

But he wasn't abandoning the old Rod completely. "How Long" showed he could still lean into soul. "Never Give Up on a Dream" – dedicated to Olympic athlete Terry Fox – proved he still had heart. And the entire album, for all its glitter and gloss, was anchored by *that* voice.

Because here's the truth: no matter what decade it was, no matter how much production changed, Rod Stewart always sounded like *Rod Stewart*. He could sing over a kazoo orchestra and still make it sound soulful. His voice – rich, rough, instantly recognizable – was his secret weapon. The times might change, but Rod? Rod *adapted*.

And he had to.

The early '80s were not kind to many of his peers. Disco was dying. Punk had burnt hot and fizzled. New wave was eating the charts. Artists who had dominated the '70s were suddenly outdated. But Rod *refused* to be irrelevant.

So he danced. He dyed. He dialed in the synths. And somehow –

incredibly – he stayed *Rod* through it all.

Still, life wasn't all chart positions and TV appearances.

His marriage to Alana Hamilton was quickly becoming a circus. The tabloids feasted on every public argument, every whispered affair. Rod, who'd once cultivated a cheeky reputation with the press, was now being hounded. It became harder to separate the man from the headlines. And Rod, though still smiling, was feeling the wear.

Being a father changed him – not instantly, but gradually. The touring life became more complicated. The desire to write confessional lyrics about love and loss clashed with the messiness of real-life relationships. And while he still played the part of the lovable rogue, cracks began to show.

But he never stopped writing.

And he never stopped *trying*.

"*Young Turks*" wasn't just a hit. It was Rod's quiet way of reminding the world – and maybe himself – that youth isn't just a number. It's a *mindset*. And no matter how many mortgages you've got or how many kids are calling you "Dad," there's always a part of you that still wants to run wild.

Rod never ran away from adulthood. But he didn't exactly let it catch him, either.

Years later, when asked about the song, Rod said it was one of his favourites – not because it was his biggest or best, but because it captured a moment. A *spirit*. That ache we all feel to break free, to chase love, to make something that's ours.

In truth, "Young Turks" is a love song. Not to a person, but to a *phase* of life. And who better to sing it than a man who, at 36, had lived harder and louder than most do in a lifetime – and still wasn't finished?

So when Rod Stewart sang, *"Time is on your side,"* he wasn't lying.

It was. And still is.

12

The First Cut Is the Deepest

"**The first cut is the deepest, baby I know...**" – *The First Cut Is the Deepest*, **Rod Stewart**

You don't become a legend of love songs without having your heart broken a few dozen times - or breaking a few along the way. And Rod Stewart, God bless him, has done both with theatrical flair, public messiness, and a curious tenderness that belies the tight trousers and tabloid headlines.

If *"The First Cut Is the Deepest"* rings true when Rod sings it, it's because he knows. He's lived that lyric - and then some.

Rod recorded his now-iconic cover of Cat Stevens' ballad in 1976. It appeared on *A Night on the Town*, an album otherwise brimming with mid-tempo soul and late-night charm. But *"First Cut"* stood out - a gut punch wrapped in violins. He didn't write it, but you'd swear he did. The way he sings that first verse - cautious, aching, full of the weight of something lost - it's not just performance. It's memory.

And that memory? It probably has a name. Or five.

Rod's romantic history is a hall of fame in its own right - models, actresses, muses, mothers of his children. But behind the headlines, there's a through-line: a man who chased love with the same reckless abandon as he chased number ones. He didn't fall - he *plunged*. And when it went wrong, it hurt in stereo.

Let's start with *Dee Harrington*.

She was a model and actress in the early '70s, striking enough to stop traffic and wise enough to see through it. Rod was smitten - until he wasn't. The relationship ended abruptly, as many of his did, and left behind enough bruised feelings to fill an album. Rod later admitted that he wasn't ready for real commitment - not then, not yet.

Then came *Britt Ekland* - Swedish beauty, former Bond girl, and arguably the first of Rod's *truly* public love affairs. They were the rock-and-roll it couple of the mid-'70s: glamorous, wild, tabloid-friendly. But behind the glitz was a volatile pairing. They fought, made up, posed for the cameras, and fought again. Rod later described the relationship as both exhilarating and exhausting.

Britt, in her memoirs, did not hold back. She painted a picture of a man who was charming, self-absorbed, and allergic to fidelity. Rod, for his part, admitted to being less than perfect - and then wrote *"Tonight's the Night"* as a kind of smirking apology. The public ate it up. The relationship, however, didn't last.

But perhaps the most significant of Rod's great loves - and heartbreaks - was *Alana Hamilton*.

Alana wasn't just a pretty face. She was smart, stylish, and already entangled in the Hollywood machine (she had previously been married to George Hamilton). She and Rod married in 1979, and for a moment, it looked like the rock star was settling down. They had two children, a picture-perfect wedding, and a Malibu mansion straight out of a glossy magazine spread.

But beneath the sunshine and the silk sheets, things began to crack. Rod was still touring constantly. The temptations were constant. And domesticity, while comforting, didn't quite fit the man who once described himself as "a rooster in a henhouse."

They divorced in 1984.

The breakup was messy, splashed across gossip columns and played out in awkward interviews. But something changed in Rod after Alana. The heartbreak stuck. It lingered. He didn't bounce back quite as fast. And his ballads - especially in the mid-'80s - began to carry a weight they hadn't before. Less performance, more confession.

Still, love wasn't done with Rod.

Kelly Emberg, a model and interior designer, became his next serious partner. They never married, but they had a daughter, Ruby, and a long, loving relationship that lasted most of the decade. Kelly brought a kind of groundedness to Rod's life - less glitz, more calm. But again, the relationship faltered under the weight of Rod's fame, his restlessness, and, reportedly, infidelity.

When they split, Rod later said he felt genuinely lost. He began to question his patterns - the chasing, the idealising, the sabotaging. It wasn't just the *first* cut that had gone deep.

Every one after had left a mark.

And then came *Rachel Hunter*.

She was 21. He was 45. The press had a field day. "She was too young. I was too in love to care," Rod later wrote. They married in 1990, and for a while, it seemed like he'd finally cracked it - longevity, stability, even serenity. They had two children and appeared regularly at events, holidays, and on the covers of Hello! magazine.

But history, as it tends to, repeated itself.

They separated in 1999 and divorced in 2006. Rod was heartbroken. Truly. He said he didn't see it coming. That it left him hollow. That he wasn't sure he'd recover.

And yet, he *did*.

Because through all the failed marriages and fractured fairy tales, Rod Stewart never gave up on love. He didn't become cynical. He didn't write bitter songs about "crazy exes." He kept singing about love the way he always had - with yearning, humour, and the knowledge that no matter how many times you fall, the right chord can still lift you.

Eventually, he met *Penny Lancaster*, the woman who would become his third wife and - by all appearances - his peace. They married in 2007 and remain together to this day. She's grounded, warm, quietly formidable. And Rod seems different around her. Softer. Happier. Still a bit cheeky, sure - but no longer chasing something he can't name.

So when Rod sings *"The First Cut Is the Deepest"* now, he sings it from a place of *knowing*. Of remembering. Of *surviving*.

He's not warning us away from love. He's simply telling the truth: the first one hurts like hell. And the ones after? They hurt in different ways.

But if you're lucky - and Rod Stewart *has* been lucky - love eventually teaches you how to bleed less, laugh more, and maybe even settle down.

Tartan trousers and all.

13

Tonight's the Night

"**D**on't say a word, my virgin child, just let your inhibitions run wild." – *Tonight's the Night (Gonna Be Alright)*, **Rod Stewart**

Rod Stewart has always known how to hold a crowd - but in 1976, he whispered into the microphone and the *whole* world leaned in.

"*Tonight's the Night*" wasn't just a hit - it was a seduction. A soft, silky, borderline scandalous slow jam that left absolutely nothing to the imagination and yet, somehow, still kept its tongue firmly in cheek. It topped the Billboard Hot 100 for eight straight weeks, became Rod's most successful US single, and sparked more than a few letters to the editor from concerned parents and morally outraged radio listeners.

And Rod? He loved every minute of it.

This was the man who had already written himself into musical history with breakup anthems and tear-streaked mandolin confessions. But now, he was turning down the lights. Taking off the boots. Pouring the wine. And crooning his way into the boudoir of a global audience.

Let's talk about *the* lyric - the one that raised more than just eyebrows: *"Don't say a word, my virgin child..."*

In 2025, it may read a bit *much*. Even in 1976, it was provocative. But at the time, it was also understood - by fans, at least - as part of the Rod Stewart persona: cheeky, audacious, suggestive. He wasn't leering. He was winking. And somehow, that made it okay.

Rod later said the line wasn't meant to be taken literally. It was theatre. Flirtation. Rock 'n' roll swagger wrapped in silk. But still, some radio stations banned it. Conservative groups complained. Rolling Stone half-scolded it, half-admired it. And Rod? He just chuckled and moved on to his next award ceremony.

The song's genius lies in its balance. For all its lyrical boldness, *"Tonight's the Night"* is musically soft - a warm, lilting groove with whispered backing vocals, a gliding melody, and that unmistakable Stewart rasp, dialled down from roar to hush. The chorus doesn't demand - it *invites*. And people came - in droves.

Backing vocals were provided by none other than *Britt Ekland*, Rod's girlfriend at the time. She delivers the breathy French whisper that closes the track - a spoken outro that tips the whole thing into full-on bedroom drama. The choice to include her wasn't just clever. It was *intimate*. The world didn't just hear

Rod singing about seduction - they heard him do it with the woman he was actually seducing.

Scandalous? A bit.

Effective? Hugely.

"*Tonight's the Night*" was the lead single from Rod's 1976 album *A Night on the Town* - a record that continued his transition into the American mainstream and further from the pub-rock roots of his Faces days. Produced by Tom Dowd and recorded in L.A., the album is slicker, fuller, more polished - but still undeniably *Rod*.

Songs like "The Killing of Georgie (Part I and II)" showed his evolving lyrical maturity - a bold, heartfelt story about a gay friend murdered in a hate crime, delivered without irony or theatricality. It was ahead of its time, tender and tragic, and still one of Rod's finest songwriting moments.

But it was "Tonight's the Night" that paid the bills. It became a staple at weddings, proms, bedroom playlists, and late-night dedications across the globe. Rod was no longer just the rock rascal with great hair - he was the king of the soft seduction. The master of the romantic wink. The balladeer of getting lucky.

Of course, not everyone bought into the charm.

Some critics rolled their eyes. Others called it sleazy. But Rod, as always, knew how to ride the line. He never came off as creepy - because he didn't *push*. He *posed*. He played. He let the listener come to him. And for millions, they did.

Offstage, Rod was deep in the Britt Ekland era – and the song mirrored their relationship: fiery, dramatic, passionate. The two were inseparable and, according to the press, constantly on the verge of either eloping or combusting. They were the Jagger and Hall of their moment – only louder, blonder, and slightly less filtered.

But for all the public flash, Rod was sharpening something else behind the scenes: control. He was no longer just riding the wave. He was *crafting* it. Every choice – from production to cover art – was calculated. He wasn't just making records. He was curating his legacy.

"Tonight's the Night" became his calling card – and not just musically. It embodied the Stewart brand: a bit dangerous, a bit ridiculous, but always delivered with enough charm to disarm even the sharpest critic.

The song has been covered, parodied, sampled, and occasionally mocked. But it's never been *forgotten*. Because for better or worse, Rod *owned* it. He wore it with the same confidence he wore his leopard trousers and open shirts. And decades later, it still makes the playlist every time someone dims the lights and reaches for a glass of wine.

Because that's Rod's gift.

He can make heartbreak sound like a hug. He can make lust sound like a lullaby. And he can sing a line like *"Let me pour you a good long drink"* with just enough gravel to make you blush – and just enough sincerity to make you believe he really means it.

Tonight's the Night wasn't just about seduction. It was about *timing*. Rod knew that music isn't just about what you say – it's *how* you say it. And in 1976, he said it better than anyone else.

So go on – put the needle on. Let the record spin. And if you feel like dancing... or something more?

Well, you know what to do.

14

Some Guys Have All the Luck

"**Some guys have all the luck, some guys have all the pain.**" – *Some Guys Have All the Luck*, **Rod Stewart**

If you only knew Rod Stewart from the headlines, you'd assume he was born in a designer crib, raised on champagne, and escorted to school by supermodels. The myth of Rod - and let's be honest, it's *legendary* - is that of a man who caught every break, charmed every beauty, and fell upward even when life was trying to trip him.

But luck? Rod Stewart *earned* his luck - and when it wasn't handed to him, he nicked it from fate with a wink and a well-timed chorus.

"*Some Guys Have All the Luck*", a cover of the 1973 Persuaders song, became one of Rod's signature hits when he released it in 1984. He turned a soulful lament into a glossy, pop-perfect anthem that seemed to mock the very idea of misfortune. Rod made it sound like a shrug and a smirk - as if to say, *"Yeah, I do have all the luck. What of it?"*

But let's rewind, because by the mid-1980s, the reality was a little more complicated.

Rod had survived disco, conquered balladry, and rebranded himself as a polished, perma-tanned pop juggernaut. The scruffy mod of the early '70s had been replaced by a man in Armani suits, driving Ferraris through Los Angeles canyons, and splitting time between homes in Malibu and London. He was photographed more often than he performed. His hair had its own column. His love life *was* the news.

From the outside, he looked invincible.

But beneath the tan and tailored threads, life wasn't quite the uninterrupted victory lap it appeared to be.

First, the fame was *relentless*. Rod had always courted the press - he understood the value of spectacle - but by the '80s, the tabloids weren't just knocking at the door. They were living in his garden. Every date, every divorce, every late-night pub sighting became front-page fodder. And Rod, no matter how seasoned, was still human.

    He later admitted that the constant attention wore him down. "It's like living in a fishbowl," he once said. "Only the water's full of gin and everyone's staring."

Then there was the challenge of staying *relevant*.

Rod wasn't just competing with his peers anymore - he was up against *generations* of artists, all younger, all hungrier. MTV had changed the game. Music was now visual. The voice wasn't enough – you needed a look, a video, a story. And Rod, now in his forties, had to prove he could still play the game.

So he did what he always did: *he adapted.*

In 1983, he released *Body Wishes* – all synths, sparkles, and stadium hooks. The critics sneered. The public bought it in droves. The lead single, "Baby Jane," became a smash, especially in the UK. Rod wasn't chasing trends – he was riding them like a man who'd invented the surfboard.

And yet, the charm came at a price.

Rod's image – the lucky playboy with women on each arm and a hit on each chart – began to overshadow the depth of his work. Some called him lightweight. Others accused him of selling out. He was too pop for the rock snobs, too rock for the pop purists, too *Rod* for anyone trying to put him in a box.

He didn't help matters by leaning into the persona. The clothes got louder. The women got younger. The interviews got cheekier. Rod was always in on the joke – but not everyone realised he was *performing.*

Still, "Some Guys Have All the Luck" felt autobiographical for a reason. Rod had a knack for falling into the right hands at the right time. A record deal here. A hit cover there. A chance encounter with a model in a hotel lobby – and suddenly she's on his arm and in the liner notes.

But behind the scenes, Rod wasn't skating through life.

There were heartbreaks – *real* ones. His split from Kelly Emberg in the late '80s left a genuine scar. They'd had a daughter together, Ruby, and for a time, Rod seemed genuinely settled. But the relationship crumbled under the weight of distance, fame, and, according to Rod, his own foolishness. He later described it as one of the few breakups he regretted - not because he lost her, but because he knew he could have done better.

There were health scares too - none public at the time, but real enough to shake his sense of invincibility. Voice fatigue, burnout, and the creeping anxiety of being *Rod Stewart* all the time.

Because here's what most people didn't see: the *work*.

Rod never phoned it in. He toured relentlessly. Rehearsed obsessively. Wrote, rewrote, and fought for creative control long after most stars of his stature had passed the baton to producers. He sweated the small stuff - the order of a setlist, the colour of a tour poster, the length of a fade-out.

He was lucky, yes - but he was *relentlessly prepared.*

That's the truth behind the lyric. The luck wasn't random. It was earned. Rod showed up. He survived every musical trend. Every wave that crashed over him, he rode it to the next hit.

And when the wave dipped? He built a boat.

He did it with humour, style, and the kind of self-awareness that turned every tabloid headline into a punchline. Even when the stories were scandalous, Rod had a way of reclaiming the narrative. *"Some Guys Have All the Luck"* wasn't just a song. It was his *motto* - delivered with a wink, a raised glass, and a knowing look that said, *"Don't hate me 'cause I'm fabulous. Hate me 'cause I'm right."*

But beneath all that glitter was grit. Rod Stewart wasn't just lucky.

He was *resilient*.

And that, as much as the hair, the hits, and the hearts he won and lost, is why he's still standing.

Because some guys *do* have all the luck. But Rod Stewart? He *earned* it - one heartbreak, one reinvention, one chart-topper at a time.

15

Forever Young

"**May the good Lord be with you, down every road you roam.**" – *Forever Young*, **Rod Stewart**

By the time Rod Stewart turned 43, the world was ready to put him on the nostalgia shelf. Another rocker entering middle age, another legend relegated to "greatest hits" tours and golf club interviews. But Rod? He wasn't having it. Instead, he took a pen, sat down with a melody, and wrote a song not about clinging to youth - but about *honouring* it.

"*Forever Young*", released in 1988 on the *Out of Order* album, wasn't a desperate plea against the passing years. It was a *blessing*. A father's prayer. A toast raised to his children, to their futures, to the beautiful mess of growing up. And when Rod Stewart sang it, it didn't sound like a rocker softening. It sounded like a man *arriving*.

The track's origin has its own twist of fate. Rod co-wrote it with Jim Cregan and Kevin Savigar, only to realise later that it bore an uncanny resemblance - lyrically and structurally - to Bob Dylan's 1974 song of the same name. Instead of a lawsuit, Rod reached out. The result? A shared songwriting credit with Dylan and a handshake that would become music-business lore. Rod called it an act of respect. Dylan, typically cryptic, didn't complain.

Rod said the song was for his kids. At the time, he had four: Sarah (his first, from a youthful relationship placed for adoption), Kimberly and Sean with Alana, and Ruby with Kelly Emberg. Fatherhood, for all his romantic escapades, had become something Rod took seriously. Not perfectly - never that - but seriously. The man who once wrote cheeky come-ons was now writing lullabies with a rock 'n' roll rasp.

"Forever Young" struck a chord with fans. It wasn't his biggest chart hit, but it became one of his most enduring. Played at graduations, weddings, memorials - any moment that marked the passing of time with hope instead of fear. Rod's voice, still unmistakably weathered and warm, gave the lyrics an authenticity few others could match.

He didn't pretend to be youthful. He *honoured* youth.

And that was Rod's new magic in the late '80s: reinvention without rejection. He didn't chase trends. He *adapted* them. His hair still reached for the heavens, but his lyrics now carried more gravity. He toured like a man half his age but interviewed like someone who'd seen it all and lived to laugh about it.

Out of Order, the album that carried "Forever Young," was a quiet triumph. Produced with Duran Duran's Andy Taylor and Chic's Bernard Edwards, it straddled pop and rock with confidence. Tracks like "Lost in You" and "My Heart Can't Tell You No" showed Rod still had chart presence. But "Forever Young" was its soul - and, for many, the soundtrack to a new Rod Stewart era.

This was no longer the man pleading with Maggie or chasing young Turks out of town. This was Rod the father. Rod the philosopher. Rod the man who'd made peace with who he was - and who he wasn't.

But don't be fooled - age didn't mean quiet.

Rod was still everywhere. He was still the king of interviews, still dropping saucy one-liners, still swanning into award shows with a supermodel on his arm. The only difference? He was *smiling more.* Less defensive. Less brash. He wasn't fighting the years. He was *singing through them.*

He spoke more openly about mistakes - the divorces, the infidelities, the way ambition had sometimes steamrolled his relationships. He talked about being a better father than he'd been a husband. He acknowledged that fame had inflated his ego and then quietly thanked his kids for bringing him back down to Earth.

In 1989, he became a grandfather - *yes, really* - when his first daughter Sarah gave birth. Rod joked about it in interviews, calling himself "Grandpa Glam," but there was a shift. The rebel was becoming the patriarch. And not begrudgingly. He *liked* it.

The '90s brought more children, more albums, and more reinvention. But "Forever Young" remained a constant - both in his live sets and in his legacy. It became the song you didn't just *listen* to, but leaned on.

When fans brought their kids to Rod Stewart concerts - and they *did* - it was often this song that brought generations together. Grandparents who danced to "Maggie May" stood next to teenagers hearing Rod for the first time. And in that chorus - *"And when you finally fly away, I'll be hoping that I served you well..."* - something timeless happened.

Rod Stewart had become a bridge - between past and future, heartbreak and healing, glamour and grit.

He wasn't trying to be young again. He was *blessing* the young.

And he wore that role as naturally as he wore tartan - with pride, with a wink, and with the understanding that staying forever young wasn't about denial.

It was about spirit.

About never losing your *spark*.

And Rod, bless him, has never lost it.

So yes, the man who once sipped Dom Pérignon on private jets and posed in leopard-print briefs is now the man who cries during his own encore of "Forever Young."

And that, perhaps more than any chart position or flashy tour, is why he endures.

Rod Stewart didn't just survive the rock 'n' roll machine. He grew up - *gracefully*, beautifully, *loudly*.

And if we're lucky, we'll do the same.

16

Rhythm of My Heart

"The rhythm of my heart is beating like a drum, with the words 'I love you' rolling off my tongue." – *Rhythm of My Heart*, **Rod Stewart**

Rod Stewart had always danced to his own beat. But in 1991, he let the drums roll from a deeper place - from somewhere old, smoky, and green. With *"Rhythm of My Heart"*, Rod wasn't just singing. He was *calling home*.

At first listen, the track is pure Stewart: a stirring vocal, sweeping production, and enough grandeur to fill a cathedral. But underneath the pop packaging beats a *Celtic heart*. Bagpipes, battlefield drums, and a melody adapted from the old Scottish folk tune *"Loch Lomond"* make this one of Rod's most profound musical homecomings.

The timing wasn't accidental.

Rod's album *Vagabond Heart*, released in March 1991, marked a turning point. After the polished pop of the '80s, Rod entered the new decade with a renewed sense of self - older, wiser, and newly in touch with his roots. He'd lived long enough to start looking *back*, not in regret, but in reverence.

And nowhere is that more evident than in "Rhythm of My Heart."

Though written by Marc Jordan and John Capek, the song felt tailor-made for Rod. It opens like a whisper on the wind, then grows - swelling into a full-throated anthem that sounds like it should be sung from mountaintops or aboard a ship heading into fog.

Rod had Scottish heritage on his father's side, and though he was born in Highgate, North London, the pull of the Highlands had always been with him. He once said, "There's something in the blood. I hear the pipes and I get goosebumps." With *"Rhythm of My Heart"*, he didn't just indulge that instinct - he *unleashed* it.

The single soared to number three in the UK and number five in the US, quickly becoming a staple in his live sets. It wasn't just a hit. It was a *statement*.

This was Rod embracing *heritage* - not just his personal ancestry, but his musical lineage. The song became a favourite among veterans, used in memorial services and patriotic events. Its themes of memory, love, and enduring connection resonated far beyond the charts.

And Rod leaned into that resonance.

In concerts, he often introduced the song with dedications to military families, to lost loved ones, to anyone holding someone in their heart from across a distance. He wasn't just singing anymore – he was *ministering*. And the audience, no matter how big, went quiet every time that first note struck.

But don't mistake this period for solemnity. Rod still had his swagger. *Vagabond Heart* also included hits like "Broken Arrow," a Robbie Robertson–penned ballad of longing and lost love, and "The Motown Song," a duet with The Temptations that proved Rod could still groove with the best of them.

Yet something had shifted.

There was *depth* now. Not just heartbreak or lust – but legacy. Rod was no longer the poster boy for disco-tinged indulgence. He was a father, a survivor, a seeker. He wasn't just entertaining crowds. He was *connecting*.

That's what "Rhythm of My Heart" captured so perfectly – the beating thread between where you've been and where you're going. The rhythm that never fades, no matter how many stadiums you sell out or supermodels you date.

In 1993, Rod took it a step further when he performed the song at President Bill Clinton's inaugural celebration. An English rock star playing a Scottish-tinged ballad for an American president – only Rod Stewart could make that make sense. And the crowd? They *roared*.

Because Rod had become something rare by the early '90s: *universal*. He could headline rock festivals, sing at royal birthdays, appear on MTV, and still bring a tear to your Nan's eye. He was *everywhere* – and everyone, somehow, claimed a little piece of him.

"Rhythm of My Heart" also became a moment of generational transmission.

Rod's children – now growing older – began to see their father not just as a celebrity, but as an *artist.* Someone with roots. Someone who was proud to carry his family's story in his voice. He'd gone from singing about skipping school to singing about the pulse of something older than all of us.

It's no coincidence that around this time, Rod began collecting rare Celtic jerseys, wearing his father's Scottish clan tartan onstage, and weaving Highland references into interviews. It wasn't for show. It was *tribute.*

To the people who made him.

To the places that shaped him.

To the rhythm that beat in his chest long before the first stadium roar.

Even now, *"Rhythm of My Heart"* holds its place in every Rod Stewart setlist. It's the emotional backbone of the evening – the point where lighters (and now iPhones) go up, voices soften, and strangers hug. Because it's not just a song. It's a *reminder.*

That home isn't a house.

It's a feeling.

And Rod, for all his wild living, wild loves, and wilder fashion, has always known where his heart beats loudest – in the stories that last, the people who matter, and the music that brings it all home.

17

Handbags & Gladrags

"They told me you missed school today, so I suggest you just throw them all away - the handbags and the gladrags..." – *Handbags and Gladrags*, **Rod Stewart**

Rod Stewart has always understood something the rest of the rock world was slow to grasp: music is a *visual* sport.

Before the MTV age demanded hair gel and neon, before Instagram turned outfits into headlines, Rod was already halfway down the catwalk - leopard print clinging to his hips, scarf trailing behind him like a comet, and hair that defied science, God, and gravity. And for Rod, it wasn't vanity. It was *performance*.

Because the gladrags? They mattered.

"*Handbags and Gladrags*," written by Mike d'Abo and recorded by Rod in 1969, was never just a song about materialism. It was about identity. About trying to belong. About the quiet ache of dressing the part when you're not sure what the part *is*. And that theme - the tension between appearance and authenticity - would weave through Rod's career like one of his beloved tartan jackets.

Rod's fashion evolution is almost its own discography. Each decade has its greatest hits - and a few delightful B-sides. In the '60s, he was the mod-in-training: slim suits, Chelsea boots, shaggy fringe, and a face that hadn't yet been lived in. By the time he joined Faces in the early '70s, his look had exploded. Shirts unbuttoned to the navel. Glitter. Stripes. Suits that looked like they were made from your grandma's curtains but somehow still *worked*.

Then came the *rooster* era.

Rod's hair, already impressive, became something mythical - a plume of blonde chaos. It wasn't a style. It was a *signature*. And it fit. Because Rod wasn't just any rocker. He was the *cheeky* one. The charmer. The guy who could wear a satin kimono and still walk into a pub without getting punched.

By the late '70s, as the solo success piled up, so did the wardrobe changes. Rod's look matured - a bit - but never dulled. He traded in flares for tailoring, but never ditched the sparkle entirely. Leopard print stayed close. So did velvet. So did that twinkle in the eye that said, *"Yes, I know this is a bit much. That's the point."*

And then came the '80s - the *Power Rod* era.

Bleach-blonde, California-tanned, often photographed on the arm of a supermodel and the hood of a convertible. Rod was the embodiment of rock star opulence: all gold chains, rolled sleeves, and dangerously short shorts. He even managed to pull off white socks with black loafers – a feat previously only attempted by moonwalking pop kings.

The press mocked it at times. "Overdressed," they said. "Too flash." But Rod never wavered. Because, again, it wasn't vanity. It was *branding*. Rod knew who he was. He knew people came to his shows not just for the music – but for the *show*. He understood theatre. And he dressed accordingly.

But fashion for Rod wasn't just performance – it was *personal*.

He often spoke about his Scottish roots influencing his wardrobe. Tartan wasn't a gimmick. It was family. He'd wear the Stewart clan tartan on stage like a superhero cape. Fans adored it. It wasn't kitsch – it was *connection*. A wink to where he came from, even when he was playing to 50,000 people in Brazil.

And then there were the suits.

Rod's tailoring in the 1990s and 2000s became sharper, cleaner, but never dull. Think Jagger meets Savile Row. He loved a bold check. A crisp white shirt. A popped collar. Always immaculate. Always a little *too* much – in the best way.

He once said, "A man should never be underdressed. And if you think you've gone too far – go further." That's the Rod Stewart rulebook in a nutshell.

It's worth saying that *nobody* has worn tight trousers longer, louder, or more proudly than Rod. Not Bowie. Not Prince. Not even Freddie. Rod made them a lifestyle. A statement. A warning. And he wore them well into his sixties, defying age, convention, and common sense.

Even as his peers faded into dad-jeans territory, Rod kept the glamour alive. And not just on stage. On red carpets, he stood out. At football matches, he brought his own kind of glitz. He was always Rod – dialled to eleven.

The real magic, though, is this: Rod's style never felt *forced*.

He wore outrageous outfits the way most people wear hoodies. Comfortably. Naturally. He never looked like he was trying to prove something. He just looked like a man who *liked looking good*. And that confidence? That's what made it work.

Of course, it helped that Rod aged well – unfairly well, some might argue. The hair remained glorious. The face, crinkled and rakish, aged like good whisky. He never tried to look 25 again. He just refined the Rod Stewart blueprint.

And in his later years, the look became almost ceremonial: sharp suit, undone shirt, dress shoes with a glint. It said, "I've been there, I've done that, and I've still got the jacket to prove it."

Because Rod Stewart, at his core, understands what *Handbags and Gladrags* really means.

It's not about clothes.

It's about *presence*.

About knowing who you are and daring to be *seen*.

And Rod? He's always been willing to be seen – loudly, proudly, and beautifully overdressed.

Long may he sparkle.

18

Sailing

"**I am sailing, I am sailing, home again, 'cross the sea."** – *Sailing*, **Rod Stewart**

It might be Rod Stewart's gentlest anthem - a prayer set to melody, a whisper above waves. When *"Sailing"* first reached the airwaves in 1975, even Rod's fiercest fans were caught off guard. Where was the swagger? The cheek? The rasping flirt in tight trousers?

What they got instead was something almost spiritual.

Written by Gavin Sutherland of The Sutherland Brothers, *"Sailing"* was never meant to be a hit. Not really. It was a quiet ballad, a folk hymn about longing, hope, and coming home. But in Rod's hands - or, more accurately, in Rod's voice - it became a lighthouse. A song not of arrival, but of return.

Released on the *Atlantic Crossing* album (a title that itself hinted at a journey both literal and emotional), *"Sailing"* was a UK chart phenomenon. It went straight to number one and stayed there for four weeks. In the US, it didn't crack the Top 40 – but that didn't matter. Rod had made something bigger than a hit. He'd made a *touchstone*.

For many fans, it was the first time Rod sounded *vulnerable*.

There's no bravado in "Sailing." No wink. No punchline. Just a man reaching. Calling out. Hoping someone's listening. It was a side of Rod we hadn't yet heard – and one that would grow louder as the years wore on.

Rod wasn't just crossing oceans in the literal sense (he had, after all, moved to America shortly before the album's release). He was crossing genres. Crossing emotional thresholds. Growing into something more than the raspy lothario.

And that's what this chapter is about.
Rod Stewart the *man* – not the hair, not the headlines, not the heartbreaks – but the quieter force who has, over the decades, proven to be kind, loyal, and surprisingly grounded.
Let's start with charity.

Rod doesn't shout about his philanthropy – and maybe that's why many don't know just how much he gives. Over the years, he's quietly donated millions to cancer research, children's hospitals, and veteran support. He's hosted charity football matches, supported the Royal National Lifeboat Institution, and donated proceeds from performances to causes close to home and far abroad.
In 2019, he revealed he'd been secretly funding a young girl's cancer treatment in the UK after hearing her story on the news.

No press release. No staged photo-op. Just Rod, quietly calling the family and offering to cover the cost. That's the man behind the curtain.

And then there's *family*.

Rod has eight children - yes, *eight* - and he's remarkably present in all their lives. From the early years of figuring out fatherhood (he'll be the first to admit he didn't always get it right), to the latter-day wisdom he shares with his younger children, Rod has evolved into something of a patriarch. Not stern, not perfect - but present.

He's talked openly about regrets - not being there enough when the older kids were growing up, letting the road come first. But he's tried, and tried hard, to bridge those gaps in adulthood. Today, the Stewart clan is a tight-knit, if eclectic, group - models, musicians, artists, students - and Rod is the heart of it.

He's even said, "Being a dad, at this age, is the best gig I've ever had." That's a long way from the man who once forgot birthdays on tour. And it's a reminder that people change - especially if they want to.

But perhaps the truest testament to Rod's soul is how *Sailing* has become part of the public consciousness in ways that transcend even his name.

It was used as the theme for the BBC documentary series *Sailor* in the late 1970s. It's been played at funerals, military memorials, and weddings. During the Falklands War, it became a sort of unofficial anthem for soldiers far from home. And during the COVID-19 pandemic, it re-emerged as a song of comfort - shared in videos, streamed at vigils, sung on balconies.

Rod noticed.

He's performed it in stripped-down arrangements, dedicating it to healthcare workers, to families separated by lockdowns, to anyone who needed to believe that they'd one day be "home again, 'cross the sea."
　Because *Sailing* isn't about ships. It's about *connection*.
　And if Rod Stewart has taught us anything, it's that behind every big stage persona is a man trying to *connect*. To his fans. To his family. To something bigger than himself.

These days, Rod's not just reflecting on his past. He's *honouring* it.

He speaks openly about ageing - not with dread, but with grace. He's still touring (at 80, no less), still recording, still outdressing men half his age. But he's doing it from a place of gratitude, not ego. The man who once strutted with a mic stand like it was an extension of his soul now stands with his arms wide - welcoming, not conquering.

And when he sings *"Sailing"* live - usually toward the end of the set - he doesn't scream it. He lets it rise. The crowd joins in. And for one moment, 20,000 strangers all seem to know exactly what he means.

We are *all* sailing.

Toward something. Away from something. Through storms, through calm. Trying to get home - wherever and whatever that is.

And Rod?

He's not just the captain anymore.

He's the song.

19

This Old Heart of Mine

"*This old heart of mine's been broke a thousand times...*" – *This Old Heart of Mine*, The Isley Brothers (covered by Rod Stewart)

Before the leopard-print, before the private jets, before the stadium anthems - there was *soul*. And if you ask Rod Stewart what made him, what taught him how to phrase a lyric, how to *feel* a verse, he won't point to a British invasion. He'll point to *Detroit*.

Rod Stewart grew up on Motown. On Sam Cooke. Otis Redding. The Temptations. The Isley Brothers. He wasn't just a fan - he was a *student*. He studied those records like sacred texts, learning how emotion could be tucked into a tremble, how a line like "*Baby, baby...*" could tell a story all on its own.

And in 1975, Rod paid homage the only way he knew how - by putting his voice to a Motown classic that had haunted him since he was a teenager.

"*This Old Heart of Mine*", originally recorded by the Isley

Brothers in 1966, was already a soul staple. But in Rod's hands, it became something else – a transatlantic love letter, filled with grit, grief, and just the right amount of British swagger.

His first version, included on *Atlantic Crossing*, was faithful but *fresh*. He didn't try to out-sing the Isleys. He brought his own ache – that husky vulnerability that made him sound like he was laughing and crying at the same time. The arrangement was tighter, the vocals raspier, the sentiment unchanged: *"I still love you..."* A declaration that never lost its punch.

But it was his 1989 duet version with Ron Isley that took it to another level.

By then, Rod was a global superstar. Ron Isley, a soul legend. Together, they didn't just re-record the song – they *celebrated* it. Two men from different musical worlds, meeting in the middle, sharing a microphone and a memory. It wasn't about who hit the highest note. It was about *respect*.

And that's what defines Rod's lifelong relationship with soul music – *respect*.

He never treated it like a costume. Never put it on for convenience. He *lived* it. He once said, "When I was busking on the streets of Paris, I was singing Sam Cooke songs, not Stones songs." Because for Rod, soul music was *the truth*. And in Rod's world, truth always comes first – right after hair product.

Throughout his career, Rod would return again and again to the well of American soul.

In 2009, he released *Soulbook* – a full album of soul classics reimagined with Rod's signature spin. He sang Smokey Robinson, Jackie Wilson, and even reunited with Mary J. Blige for a crackling version of *"You Make Me Feel Brand New."* It wasn't trend-chasing. It was a man revisiting his roots - with gratitude, not nostalgia.

But the beauty of Rod's connection to soul isn't just in the covers.

It's in the *influence*.

Listen to *"You're In My Heart"*, *"Reason to Believe"*, even *"I Don't Want to Talk About It"* - and you'll hear it. The phrasing. The ache. The *pleading*. All lifted straight from the Marvin Gaye playbook, filtered through a London accent and a life lived at full tilt.

Rod has said many times that his dream would've been to record for Motown in the '60s. And while that dream never quite came true, he carried Motown's spirit into every era of his career - adapting it to rock, to pop, even to big band swing.

But no matter the arrangement, that old soul heartbeat always pulsed underneath.

It's what gave Rod the edge over his contemporaries. What made him more than just a raspy voice and a good haircut. Soul gave him *depth*. A second dimension. The ability to sing about heartbreak without sounding pitiful, about longing without sounding weak.

When Rod sang *"This Old Heart of Mine"*, he wasn't just covering a song. He was admitting something: that even behind the fame, the women, the endless wardrobe changes - there was a man who still missed someone. Who still cared. Who still *felt*.

And that honesty – that soul – is why the song endures.

It's still in the live set. Still brings the house down. Still makes couples slow dance in stadium aisles. Because everyone, at some point, has loved someone who didn't love them back the same way. And Rod, God love him, has the courage to keep singing about it.

In that way, soul music didn't just influence Rod Stewart.

It *saved* him.

From arrogance. From detachment. From becoming just another icon phoning it in. Soul kept him *connected*. To his emotions. To his fans. To the idea that music, at its best, is *shared experience*.

And it's fitting that one of his most iconic tributes to the genre is called *This Old Heart of Mine*.

Because that's Rod – always heart first.

A little bruised. A little wiser. Still beating like a Motown backbeat.

And still wide open.

20

Baby Jane

"**Baby Jane, don't leave me hanging on the line…**" –
Baby Jane, **Rod Stewart**

By 1983, Rod Stewart had conquered just about everything a rocker could dream of: platinum records, sold-out tours, a wardrobe that required its own postcode. But something strange was happening. The kids were starting to look elsewhere. The world was changing - and fast. Punk had snarled its way through the charts, New Wave was sparkling on MTV, and Rod?

Well, Rod was *ready*.

Enter: *Baby Jane* - a song that didn't just revive Rod's pop credentials, it *reinvented* them. Released in May 1983, it would become his last UK number-one single to date, topping the charts for three weeks and strutting into the canon with synths blazing. This wasn't the Rod of "Maggie May" or even "Do Ya Think I'm Sexy?" This was *Power Suit Rod*. And he meant business.

But let's backtrack.

The early '80s hadn't exactly been kind to Rod, creatively. Albums like *Foolish Behaviour* (1980) and *Tonight I'm Yours* (1981) had solid moments, but the critics were circling. Was Rod too glossy? Too Americanised? Too busy being photographed with actresses to focus on songwriting?

Rod, as ever, didn't flinch. He simply hit the studio - with longtime collaborators Jim Cregan and Kevin Savigar - and cooked up *Body Wishes*, an album that would split fans and critics alike, but deliver one undeniable banger: *Baby Jane*.

From the opening drum machine to the slick, arpeggiated synth line, the song screams *'80s energy*. But at the heart of it, lyrically and vocally, is vintage Rod - a kiss-off wrapped in vulnerability. He's angry, sure. But he's *hurt*, too. And you feel every syllable.

"You're a teaser, a trickster..." - he growls.

And we believe him.

"Baby Jane" might not be about one specific person (though it's tempting to guess - the list of possible Jane-like muses in Rod's love life is long), but it *feels* like it is. That's the Rod Stewart genius: even when it's general, it's personal. He could be singing about your breakup - and somehow, it sounds better with a sax solo.

Visually, the *Baby Jane* era was peak '80s Rod. The hair got higher. The suits got shinier. The dance moves - well, let's just say he didn't let rhythm get in the way of enthusiasm. On *Top of the Pops*, he twirled and pointed like a man possessed by Duran

Duran's wardrobe manager. And we *loved* it.

Critics, naturally, weren't always kind. *Body Wishes* was called synthetic. Overproduced. Lacking the rawness of early Stewart. But they missed the point. Rod wasn't trying to be raw anymore. He was playing the game – and playing it well.

"Baby Jane" wasn't about staying stuck in the past. It was about proving he could thrive in the *now*. He didn't just want to be a legend. He wanted to be *current*. And for that summer in 1983, he was *everywhere*. The song dominated radio. The video was on constant rotation. And suddenly, Rod wasn't just your mum's favourite anymore – the kids were back on board.

And what of the song itself?

At 4 minutes and 43 seconds, it's tightly constructed, with a killer chorus and a bridge that punches. The production is polished – full of gated reverb and synth stabs, everything you want from a glossy '80s hit. But it's Rod's vocal that seals it. His voice, by now seasoned and lived-in, cuts through the mix with authority. He wasn't trying to sound young. He was *owning* his sound in a new context.

And fans? They responded.

"Baby Jane" topped the UK charts and became a European hit, too. It was less successful in the US, but it reminded everyone that Rod Stewart was a *chameleon* – and one who could thrive under any spotlight.

But more than that, it marked a kind of late-career *pivot point*.

Rod wasn't just about albums anymore. He was about *moments* – singles that struck a chord, that stuck in your head, that earned their spot in the encore. "Baby Jane" became one of those. It's still a crowd-pleaser in live shows, a chance for the band to loosen up and for Rod to let loose. It's flirtatious. It's fiery. It's fun.

And like so much of Rod's catalogue, it's aged better than anyone predicted. Play it now and it still pops. It doesn't try to be timeless - and maybe that's why it *is*.

In interviews, Rod's spoken about "Baby Jane" with real affection. He knows it's not "Mandolin Wind" or "Reason to Believe." It's not meant to be. It's a *banger*. A strut. A shoulder-pad in song form. And he wears it proudly.

Because here's the thing about Rod Stewart: he's never been afraid to evolve.

Folk? Done it. Rock? Owned it. Disco? Tried it on for size. Synth-pop? Bring it. He doesn't cling to one era. He moves. He *dances*. Sometimes awkwardly, always confidently.

"Baby Jane" was Rod proving - once again - that you can grow older without growing irrelevant. That you can wear a white blazer and still sound cool. That heartbreak, when filtered through a chorus that explodes like a glitter cannon, is *pure joy*.

And let's face it: there's a little "Baby Jane" in all of us.

The one that got away. The one we're not over. The one we're still writing songs about in the
   back of our mind.

Rod just had the guts - and the groove - to put it on vinyl.

21

You're in My Heart

"*You're in my heart, you're in my soul, you'll be my breath should I grow old...*" – *You're in My Heart*, **Rod Stewart**

By now, we've danced through the decades with Rod Stewart - from the smoky pubs of London to the flashing lights of L.A., from heartbreak to hair spray, and everywhere in between. We've watched him fall in love, fall apart, and fall right back on his feet, always with a wink, a whistle, and a voice that cracked beautifully right where the truth lived.

But here, at the edge of our journey, it's not the biggest hits or wildest nights that echo the loudest.

It's this.

"*You're in My Heart*", released in 1977, wasn't his flashiest single. It didn't come with leopard print or a disco beat. But it came with honesty - a soft-rock ballad penned at the height of his superstardom that sounded like it was meant for the quiet of your living room. A love letter set to music.

Written for then-partner Britt Ekland, it became something bigger than its original muse. It became Rod's anthem of devotion. Not just to a woman, but to *life itself* - to family, to football, to music, to the fans. To *us*.

And if you're still reading, chances are... he's in your heart too.

Rod's story isn't just about a career. It's about *connection*. He never claimed to be perfect. He never hid the mess. But in a world that loves a comeback, Rod never really left. He kept showing up - album after album, tour after tour, heartbreak after heartbreak - offering us another chapter, another laugh, another truth we didn't know we needed.

In later years, Rod took stock. He wrote two autobiographies (because one simply couldn't contain all the tartan). He revisited the Great American Songbook, not out of nostalgia, but reverence - showing the same soul he once borrowed from Sam Cooke and Otis Redding now belonged entirely to him.

He survived cancer. Twice. And he came back stronger, not just in voice, but in perspective. His interviews got more candid. His jokes got even funnier. And his concerts? Still a party - but with more stories between songs, more eye contact, more *gratitude*.

Fatherhood mellowed him. Grandfatherhood humbled him. But the Rod Stewart of today - still touring, still writing, still squeezing into glorious tailoring - remains unmistakably *Rod*. A little wiser. A little gentler. Still full of cheek. Still full of charm.

He's not just in our hearts because he sang us through breakups and makeups and Friday nights.

He's there because he *let us in*.

He showed us what it means to live boldly. To love publicly. To screw up gloriously. To walk through life with a soundtrack you *sing at the top of your lungs*. And even now, at eighty, he's not fading. He's *shining*.

"You're in My Heart" closes every show now like a prayer. Fans sway. Couples hold hands. Grown men cry. Rod steps forward - hand over chest, voice steady as ever - and sings not at the crowd, but *to* them.

Because this song isn't just a declaration. It's a *thank you*.

To the fans who stayed.

To the bandmates who played.

To the lovers who left and the ones who remained.

To every soul who ever saw a bit of themselves in a Stewart lyric.

And to us, here, now - reading this.

Rod Stewart is more than his records. He's a feeling.

And that's why he'll always be in our hearts.

Forever young.

Forever loud.

Forever Rod.

22

Fan Fun

Which Rod Stewart Song Are You?

Take the quiz, circle your answers, and discover your inner Rod anthem...

1. What's your ideal Saturday night?
A) Dancing till dawn, dressed to impress
B) A long drive with your favourite playlist
C) Candlelit dinner and heartfelt conversation
D) Football, pints, and mates – in that order
E) Flicking through old photo albums and weeping, gloriously

2. Your fashion motto?
A) Leopard print is a neutral
B) Denim is forever
C) Vintage, classic, and effortlessly cool
D) Kit first, questions later

E) Slightly overdressed, always under emotional repair

3. Your love life in one phrase?
   A) Complicated but cinematic
   B) "Can't live with 'em, can't write hit singles without 'em"
   C) Quiet, steady, soulful
   D) Loyal through and through
   E) "I still love them... from a safe emotional distance"

4. Pick a Rod lyric that speaks to your soul:
   A) "Some guys have all the luck..."
   B) "Tonight's the night, it's gonna be alright..."
   C) "You're in my heart, you're in my soul..."
   D) "We are sailing, home again..."
   E) "I don't wanna talk about it..."

5. Your most prized possession is:
   A) Your record collection
   B) Your passport and a packed bag
   C) A handwritten love letter from 1992
   D) Your season ticket
   E) A perfectly curated breakup playlist

Results:

Mostly A's – "Do Ya Think I'm Sexy?"

You're glitz, glam, and always the life of the party. You're unafraid to strut your stuff, flirt across a dance floor, or rock a rhinestone jacket with meaning. Beneath the sass? A heart of gold and surprisingly good relationship advice.

Mostly B's – "Young Turks"

You're restless, romantic, and probably overdue for a spontaneous road trip. You believe in second chances, loud music, and the kind of love that runs away with you. Adventure *is* your middle name.

Mostly C's – "You're in My Heart"

Loyal, loving, and deeply sentimental, you're the warm cup of tea in Rod's discography. You cry at weddings, still send birthday cards, and know the power of a well-timed slow dance.

Mostly D's – "Sailing"

You've got depth, direction, and a strong moral compass. You're often the grounding force in your circle - steady and sure, with dreams bigger than the sea. You've been through storms, and you still believe in home.

Mostly E's – "I Don't Want to Talk About It"

A romantic soul with a bittersweet streak. You feel things *deeply*, cry at songs with string sections, and love like it's a vintage wine - carefully, slowly, but all the way. You may not say much, but your playlists speak volumes.

23

Thank You (for the Music, the Hair, and the Heart)

If you've made it this far, I owe you more than a signed tour programme and a pint at Celtic Park. Thanks for walking through the decades with me - the glory, the gravel, the gladrags, and the grooves. Rod Stewart isn't just a legend because of the records he's sold or the women he's serenaded - he's a legend because of *you*. Because fans like us kept turning up the volume, even when critics turned up their noses.

Writing this book has been a love letter, a mixtape, a backstage pass to a life lived loud. And whether you're here for the early mod years, the disco flirtations, or the stripped-down soul of his later records - I hope you found a piece of your own story tucked somewhere between the tartan and the truth.

Now, if you're feeling the rhythm of *your* heart (and still humming along to "Maggie May" like it's 1971), I've got one tiny favour to ask:

🎤 *Leave a review.*

Seriously. A few kind words on the platform where you bought this book - whether it's a star rating, a memory of your first Rod gig, or just "Bobby Gallagher made me cry over leopard print" - helps more than you know.

Rod gave us decades of music.

Let's give him a chorus of five-star thank-yous.

Until next time - keep your mic stand spinning, your shirts unbuttoned (tastefully), and your soul singing.

Yours in rasps and romance,

Bobby Gallagher

24

Rod Stewart Discography

Studio Albums

1. *An Old Raincoat Won't Ever Let You Down* (1969)
2. *Gasoline Alley* (1970)
3. *Every Picture Tells a Story* (1971)
4. *Never a Dull Moment* (1972)
5. *Smiler* (1974)
6. *Atlantic Crossing* (1975)
7. *A Night on the Town* (1976)
8. *Foot Loose & Fancy Free* (1977)
9. *Blondes Have More Fun* (1978)
10. *Rod Stewart* (1980)
11. *Tonight I'm Yours* (1981)
12. *Body Wishes* (1983)
13. *Camouflage* (1984)
14. *Every Beat of My Heart* (1986)
15. *Out of Order* (1988)
16. *Vagabond Heart* (1991)

17. *A Spanner in the Works* (1995)
18. *When We Were the New Boys* (1998)
19. *Human* (2001)
20. *It Had to Be You: The Great American Songbook* (2002)
21. *As Time Goes By: The Great American Songbook, Volume II* (2003)
22. *Stardust: The Great American Songbook, Volume III* (2004)
23. *Thanks for the Memory: The Great American Songbook, Volume IV* (2005)
24. *Still the Same... Great Rock Classics of Our Time* (2006)
25. *Soulbook* (2009)
26. *Fly Me to the Moon... The Great American Songbook Volume V* (2010)
27. *Time* (2013)
28. *Another Country* (2015)
29. *Blood Red Roses* (2018)
30. *The Tears of Hercules* (2021)

Key Compilation Albums

- *Sing It Again Rod* (1973)
- *Greatest Hits Vol. 1* (1979)
- *Storyteller – The Complete Anthology: 1964–1990* (1989)
- *The Very Best of Rod Stewart* (2001)
- *The Rod Stewart Sessions 1971–1998* (2009)
- *You're in My Heart: Rod Stewart with the Royal Philharmonic Orchestra* (2019)

Live Albums

- *Absolutely Live* (1982)
- *Unplugged...and Seated* (1993)
- *Live the Life Tour* (2013)
- *Live in Hyde Park: One Night Only* (2016)
- *The Royal Philharmonic Concert (Live)* (2019)

Notable Collaborations & Duets

- "This Old Heart of Mine" (with Ronald Isley)
- "All for Love" (with Bryan Adams and Sting – *The Three Musketeers* soundtrack, 1993)
- "Forever Young" (inspired by Dylan, blessed by Dylan)
- "Have I Told You Lately" (live version from *Unplugged...and Seated*)
- "You Make Me Feel Brand New" (with Mary J. Blige, *Soulbook*)

Printed in Dunstable, United Kingdom